DOMAIN 1

CLOUD COMPUTING CONCEPTS AND ARCHITECTURES

CCSK Practice Tests – Cloud Security Alliance (CSA) Security Guidance v4

1. Alice runs a small software development company, and wants to use a cloud environment to install, test, and modify applications across a number of operating systems (OSs). Which cloud service model is probably best for her purposes?

    A. IaaS

    B. PaaS

    C. SaaS

    D. Grimbo

2. You are the security officer for a small business that stores medical records for wealthy celebrities; your clients pay premium prices for the highest possible security. Your company is considering moving from a traditional, on-premise data center to the cloud. Senior management has asked for your recommendation on which cloud deployment model to use. You recommend:

    A. public cloud

    B. private cloud

    C. community cloud

    D. hybrid cloud

3. In an IaaS model, which party is responsible for ensuring that the operating system (OS) on the guest virtual machine (VM) is configured, maintained, and patched properly?

   A. cloud provider

   B. regulator

   C. auditor

   D. cloud customer

4. Which of the following terms is not used to describe cloud computing, in either the ISO or NIST definitions?

   A. elastic

   B. shared resources

   C. frangible

   D. self-service

5. Which of the following practices distinguishes cloud computing from a traditional environment?

   A. virtualization

   B. monetization

   C. abstraction

   D. orchestration

6. Which of the following elements distinguishes cloud computing from a traditional environment?

   A. multitenancy

   B. heuristics

   C. planning

   D. resiliency

7. Which of the following elements is typically not an element of cloud computing?

    A. multitenancy

    B. isolation

    C. segregation

    D. subsidization

8. Which of the following is not a typical cloud deployment model, as defined by NIST and ISO?

    A. hybrid

    B. community

    C. private

    D. isolated

9. According to the Cloud Security Alliance, most modern APIs (application programming interfaces) use _____.

    A. electricity

    B. native architecture

    C. REST (representational state transfer)

    D. FTP (file transfer protocol)

10. Which element of the CSA cloud logical model includes the data in file storage?

    A. applistructure

    B. infostructure

    C. metastructure

    D. infrastructure

11. Which element of the CSA cloud logical model defines the difference

between cloud and traditional computing?

    A. applistructure

    B. infostructure

    C. metastructure

    D. infrastructure

12. Which of the following is not a cloud security model recommended by the Cloud Security Alliance (CSA)?

    A. NIST SP (National Institute of Standards and Technology Special Publication) 500-299 Cloud Computing Security Reference Architecture

    B. CSA Enterprise Architecture

    C. Nebulous Consolidated Framework (NCF)

    D. ISO/IEC (International Standards Organization/International Electrotechnical Commission) 27017 Information technology – Security techniques – Code of practice for information security controls based on ISO/IEC 27002 for cloud services.

13. According to the cloud computing shared responsibility model, who is responsible for the security of the hardware in an SaaS environment?

    A. The cloud provider

    B. The cloud customer

    C. The regulator

    D. The auditor

14. Which of the following are tools provided by the CSA to help both cloud providers and cloud customer meet regulatory compliance requirements? Choose all that apply.

    A. The Cloud Controls Matrix (CCM)

    B. The Consensus Assessments Initiative Questionnaire (CAIQ)

C. The Diffie-Hellman algorithm

D. The Artichoke Incorporation Model

15. Put the following cloud security process steps in the correct order:

    A. Identify control gaps.

    B. Identify necessary security and compliance requirements, and any existing controls.

    C. Define the architecture.   p 23

    D. Manage changes over time.

    E. Select your cloud provider, service, and deployment models.

    F. Design and implement controls to fill the gaps.

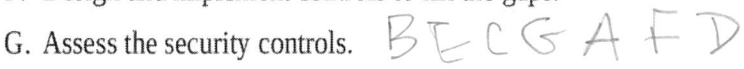

    G. Assess the security controls.   B E C G A F D

16. The Cloud Security Alliance (CSA) Security Guidance v4 contains 14 domains. The two major categories of domains are [choose two]:

    A. operations

    B. governance

    C. maintenance

    D. technology

17. Which of the following is not a critical focus area in the domains of the Cloud Security Alliance (CSA) Security Guidance v4?

    A. Governance and enterprise risk management

    B. Legal issues: contracts and electronic discovery

    C. Continuous monitoring and observation

    D. Compliance and audit management

18. Which of the following is not a critical focus area in the domains of the Cloud Security Alliance (CSA) Security Guidance v4?

A. Infrastructure security

B. Malleable formations ✗

C. Virtualization and containers

D. Related technologies

19. Which of the following tools can be used to evaluate various cloud service providers?

    A. Sarbanes-Oxley (SOX)

    B. General Data Protection Regulation (GDPR)

    ✓ C. Consensus Assessments Initiative Questionnaire (CAIQ)

    D. The STRIDE model

20. According to the Cloud Security Alliance (CSA) Security Guidance v4, it is important for the CCSK candidate to understand how _____ and _____ impact security [choose two].

    A. financing

    B. abstraction 1

    C. technology

    D. automation 2

21. A cloud provider offering database services is most likely utilizing the _____ service model.

    A. IaaS

    B. PaaS ✓

    C. SaaS

    D. Las

22. According to the Cloud Security Alliance (CSA) Security Guidance v4, if an attacker gets access to your _____, they could acquire full remote access to your cloud enterprise.

A. cloud management plane ✓

B. endpoint device

C. username list

D. hashed password file

23. The NIST (National Institute of Standards and Technology) definition of cloud computing includes _____ essential characteristics, _____ service models, and _____ deployment models.

   A. 5, 3, 4 ✓
   B. 6, 2, 4
   C. 5, 5, 5
   D. 3, 4, 2
   E. 6, 4, 3
   F. 4, 5, 4

24. According to the Cloud Security Alliance (CSA) Security Guidance v4, in a multitenant environment, customers should be _____ and _____ from each other [choose two].

   A. isolated ✓
   B. insulated
   C. constrained
   D. segregated ✓
   E. invoiced
   F. allocated

25. According to the Cloud Security Alliance (CSA) Security Guidance v4, what's the most important security consideration for any cloud project?

   A. knowing who is responsible for what ✓
   B. personal privacy

C. physical protection of the underlying architecture

D. preventing electronic surveillance

DOMAIN 2
GOVERNANCE AND ENTERPRISE RISK MANAGEMENT

CCSK Practice Tests – Cloud Security Alliance (CSA) Security Guidance v4

26. In a hierarchy of organizational priority, which of the following is the least influential?

    A. governance

    B. enterprise risk management

    C. information risk management

    D. information security ✓

27. Which of the following is impossible to outsource?

    A. information technology management

    B. responsibility for governance ✓

    C. financial management

    D. audit review

28. Cloud providers try to manage costs and enable capabilities by _____.

    A. leveraging economies of scale ✓

    B. arbitrating contract breaches

C. facilitating customer service

D. enhancing public perception

29. Two ways a cloud customer can address governance gaps in the contract include _____ and _____ [select two].

    A. refuse service

    B. adjust internal processes ✓

    C. accept risks ✓

    D. appeal to regulators

30. What is the customer's only guarantee of any level of service or commitment from the provider?

    A. due diligence

    B. the contract ✓

    C. regulatory supervision

    D. physical force

31. When reviewing external assessments and audits of a potential cloud provider, it is critical that the customer understands the _____.

    A. current rate of inflation

    B. type of hypervisor currently in use at the cloud data center

    C. competitive market

    D. scope of the assessment/audit ✓

32. Which of the following is not typically considered when determining whether a particular auditor/audit firm is trustworthy?

    A. past performance

    B. number of auditors involved ✗

    C. accreditation/credentials/certification

D. reputation

33. Which of the following is an assurance program for cloud customers to review assessments of various cloud providers?

    A. the CSA Cloud Controls Matrix (CCM)

    B. the CSA Security, Trust, and Risk (STAR) Registry ✓ ?

    C. the CSA Consensus Assessments Initiative Questionnaire (CAIQ)

    D. the CSA Oblique Inference Program (OIP)

34. Which of the following best describes the way risk is managed in the cloud?

    A. the Bell-LaPadula Model

    B. covert channel

    C. the shared responsibilities model ✓

    D. total outsource of risk management

35. Enterprise risk management in the cloud often depends on _____ and _____ [select two].

    A. documentation ✓

    B. financial equity

    C. public interest

    D. good contracts ✓

    E. physical distance

36. Who determines the amount of risk tolerance an organization should have?

    A. regulators

    B. senior management ✓

C. cloud providers

D. government officials

37. Which common cloud service model typically requires a well-negotiated contract between the provider and customer?

   A. IaaS

   B. PaaS

   C. SaaS ✓

   D. BaaS

38. SaaS providers are typically either _____ or _____ companies.

   A. very large or very small ✓

   B. domestic or foreign

   C. technological or administrative

   D. inflated or conflated

39. Which common cloud service model is the nearest approximation of a traditional data center?

   A. IaaS ✓

   B. PaaS

   C. SaaS

   D. QaaS

40. What causes the inflexibility of contracts in the public cloud deployment model?

   A. hypervisors

   B. regulators

   C. inversion

D. multitenancy ✓

41. When using a hybrid cloud model, the customer must ensure that the _____ spans both environments.

    A. physical network

    B. interface mesh

    C. observance criteria

    D. governance ✓

42. Which of the following is a significant factor of enterprise risk in a public cloud environment?

    A. elevated exposure to intellectual property

    B. regulators inspect cloud resources faster

    C. less physical access to infrastructure ✓

    D. increased electrical power usage

43. Cloud providers are constantly updating and upgrading the technology and processes in their data centers, in order to enhance product delivery, customer needs, and profitability. This affects customers' enterprise risk management, because it will require _____.

    A. joint approval of all actions

    B. increased customer engagement to ensure adherence to contracts (beyond the initial contract signing) ✓

    C. additional use of contract staff

    D. more personal devices used to interact with the cloud environment

44. Which of the following is true about enterprise risk management in the cloud?

    A. customers can transfer privacy risk to providers

B. customers can transfer risk management to providers

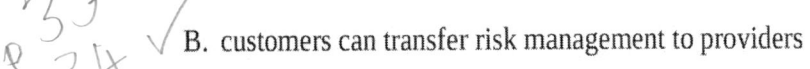

C. providers can transfer privacy risk to customers

D. providers can accept risk on behalf of customers

45. Which of the following is not an option for managing risk?

    A. avoid

    B. articulate

    C. transfer

    D. accept

46. Put the supplier assessment process in the correct order.

    A. Review their security program and documentation.

    B. Request or acquire documentation.

    C. Review any legal, regulatory, contractual, and jurisdictional requirements for both the provider and yourself.

    D. Separately evaluate the overall provider, such as finances/stability, reputation, and outsourcers.

    E. Evaluate the contracted service in the context of your information assets.

47. Which mechanism is most often used to transfer risk?

    A. regulation

    B. governance

    C. insurance

    D. postulation

48. Which of the following is not a best practice for cloud customers?

    A. periodically review supplier assessments/audits to ensure they are up to date

B. don't assume that multiple services offered by a provider all meet the same standard

C. automate reviews whenever possible

D. renegotiate contracts after every review

49. After controls are applied to a particular risk, the remaining risk is called "_____ risk."

    A. inflammatory

    B. inherent

    C. transferred

    D. residual

50. Which of the following untrue/incorrect about cloud service contracts?

    A. the customer should review contracts before entering agreements with cloud providers

    B. if the customer is not allowed to negotiate contract terms (for instance, with a major public cloud provider), the customer should not use that provider

    C. even if the customer cannot negotiate contract terms (for instance, with a major provider of public cloud services), that provider might still be useful, and the customer might still use that provider

    D. customers can use additional controls (such as encryption or monitoring) to address specific risks

DOMAIN 3
LEGAL ISSUES, CONTRACTS, AND ELECTRONIC DISCOVERY

CCSK Practice Tests – Cloud Security Alliance (CSA) Security Guidance v4

51. Which of the following is probably the best way to address your organization's particular legal issues?

    A. Get an account for a legal review service, such as Westlaw or Lexis/Nexis

    B. Perform personal research on the Internet

    C. Download the laws of each country where you organization operates

    ✓ D. Consult with an attorney in the jurisdiction(s) where your organization operates

52. Who is the original owner of privacy data?

    A. The subject ✓

    B. The processor

    C. The controller

    D. The regulator

53. Countries/regions may have either _____ or _____ privacy laws [select two].

A. optional

B. omnibus ✓

C. hierarchical

D. advantageous

E. placid

F. internal

G. sectoral ✓

54. Under many privacy laws, personal data can only be sent to another country if the receiving country's laws offer _____.

   A. reciprocity

   B. adequate level of protection ✓

   C. cash awards

   D. full encryption and secure data storage

55. In some countries, privacy laws require that data be stored _____.

   A. in plain text

   B. within the country's borders ✓

   C. in the cloud

   D. in a proprietary format

56. Which country/region does not have an omnibus personal privacy law?

   A. Australia

   B. The European Union

   C. Argentina

   D. The United States ✗ federal instead

57. Which country/region does not have an omnibus personal privacy law?

A. China

B. Canada

C. Japan *— sectoral*

D. Chile

58. Which of the following is not true about the European Union's (EU'S) General Data Protection Regulation (GDPR)?

    A. it applies to all entities processing EU citizen personal data

    ✗ B. it only applies within the EU and the Commonwealth

    C. it treats personal privacy as a fundamental human right

    D. it regulates cross-border data transfer to countries outside the EU

59. According to the European Union's (EU'S) General Data Protection Regulation (GDPR), breaches involving personal data must be reported to authorities within _____ of detection.

    ✓ A. 72 hours   p 42

    B. one week

    C. one day

    D. 24 hours

60. Any company violating the European Union's (EU'S) General Data Protection Regulation (GDPR) may face monetary penalties of up to _____.

    A. 100 million euros

    B. 4% of that company's annual global gross revenue ✓

    C. half of its operating capital   ≤ $20m

    D. 10,000 euros per customer affected

61. Contractual obligations for companies operating in the cloud might derive from all of the following except _____.

A. a terms of service statement

B. a privacy statement

C. contracts the company has with third parties

D. international law ✗   p 45

62. If an organization contracts with a cloud provider to manage personal data, who is generally liable for any damages caused by unauthorized disclosure of that data, under most privacy laws?

A. the cloud provider

B. the data subject

C. regulators

D. the organization ✓

63. Under the European Union's (EU's) General Data Protection Regulation (GDPR), which of the following is the most important characteristic of the data subject's interaction with the data controller?

A. availability

B. business

C. consent ✓

D. decryption

64. Which of the following is perhaps the best reason to conduct due diligence?

A. enhance profitability

B. reduce liability ✓

C. raise public esteem

D. defeat dedicated attackers

65. Which part of an audit/assessment describes the features and services included in that audit/assessment?

A. the introduction

B. the executive summary

C. the scope ✓

D. the lessons learned

66. Contracts can generally protect from all the following types of risk except _____.

   A. legal

   B. reputational

   C. commercial

   ✓ D. hacking

67. A thorough review of all contract elements (such as service agreements, schedules, and appendices) is an especially important form of due diligence in cloud managed service arrangements, because many cloud services are _____.

   A. excessive

   B. non-negotiable ✓

   C. ludicrous

   D. illegal

68. Third-party audits and attestations are often used to demonstrate a cloud provider's _____ with a given standard.

   A. agreement

   B. compliance ✓

   C. contract

   D. membership

69. What is the term used to describe a legal process for opposing counsel to acquire private data/documents for purposes of litigation?

A. seizure

B. invasion

C. discovery ✓

D. surveillance

70. In some jurisdictions, if one party to a lawsuit loses, modifies, or deletes information that could be used as evidence in the suit, the jury may be instructed to _____.

✓ A. presume that the evidence would be the worst possible information for that party's case

B. determine what the missing information contained from whatever partial information is available

C. ignore any arguments that suggest the missing information might affect the suit in any way

D. not consider the missing information at all

71. In order to present all relevant and probative data pertinent to a legal case, a cloud customer might be required to _____ data.

A. destroy

B. overpreserve ✓

C. copy

D. interpret

72. Bit-by-bit imaging of cloud data for forensic purposes is generally _____.

A. required by law

B. up to the cloud customer

C. extremely expensive

D. difficult or impossible ✓

73. In a cloud environment, it is not likely that a requesting party in litigation will have _____ the customer's IT enterprise.

    A. awareness of

    B. direct access to ✓

    C. familiarity with

    D. working knowledge of

74. In order to reliably challenge a legal order to disclose data belonging to a cloud customer, it is desirable to include a requirement for _____ in the contract.

    ✓ A. the cloud provider to notify the customer of any legal requests

    B. the cloud provider to deny any legal requests

    C. the cloud provider to resist any search or seizure attempts

    D. the cloud provider to retain counsel

75. Among other resources, the Cloud Security Alliance (CSA) recommends _____ for additional knowledge about legal evidentiary matters.

    A. the Open Web Application Security Project (OWASP)

    B. the Sedona Conference ✓ p53

    C. your local library

    D. waiting for instructions from the court where litigation occurs

DOMAIN 4
COMPLIANCE AND AUDIT MANAGEMENT

CCSK Practice Tests – Cloud Security Alliance (CSA) Security Guidance v4

76. _____ existing regulation were written to account for virtualized environments or cloud deployments.

   A. Most

   B. No

   C. Few ✓

   D. All

77. Which aspects of cloud computing make traditional audit approaches difficult [select two]?

   A. resiliency

   B. virtualized ✓

   C. self-service

   D. metered service

   E. distributed ✓

   F. physical

   p 54

78. Audits typically may be _____ or _____.

A. fast or slow

B. internal or external ✓

C. nocturnal or diurnal

D. legal or illegal

79. In the cloud computing model, who is ultimately responsible for the ensuring customer compliance with a given standard/regulation?

    A. the cloud provider

    B. the cloud customer ✓   p55

    C. the regulator

    D. the data subject

80. Cloud customers will typically have to rely on _____ in order to understand a provider's compliance alignment and gaps.

    A. regulator reports

    B. public news articles

    C. personal investigation

    D. third-party attestations ✓

81. Alice is the security manager for a mid-sized retail. Alice's company contracts with a cloud provider for an IaaS environment, then builds an environment of virtual servers and an application to allow clientele to perform online ordering and credit card payment. The cloud provider has documentation proving that the provider is currently compliant with the Payment Card Industry Data Security Standard (PCI-DSS).

    What is the term used to describe the relationship between Alice's company and the provider, in terms of PCI-DSS compliance?

    A. compliance inheritance ✓

    B. nonregulated inversion

    C. regulatory capture

D. essential proffering

82. Alice is the security manager for a mid-sized retail. Alice's company contracts with a cloud provider for an IaaS environment, then builds an environment of virtual servers and an application to allow clientele to perform online ordering and credit card payment. The cloud provider has documentation proving that the provider is currently compliant with the Payment Card Industry Data Security Standard (PCI-DSS).

Who is responsible for ensuring that Alice's company's virtual machines and application are compliant with PCI-DSS?

    A. the PCI Council

    B. Alice's company ✓

    C. the cloud provider

    D. Alice's ISP

83. Which of the following is not typically used for third-party attestation in the cloud?

    A. the General Data Protection Regulation (GDPR) of the European Union (EU)

    ✓ B. the Certified Information System Security Professional (CISSP) certification from ISC2

    C. the Payment Card Industry Data Security Standard (PCI DSS)

    D. the System and Organization Controls (SOC) reports of the American Institute of Certified Public Accountants (AICPA)

84. Why is it crucial for cloud customers to understand the scope and limitations of each certification, audit, and attestation report offered by the cloud provider?

    A. the customer may determine those are insufficient, and decide to perform their own audit of the cloud provider's data center

    B. some audits may be illegal in the customer's jurisdiction

C. not all features and services within a given cloud provider are necessarily compliant and certified/audited with respect to all regulations and standards

D. the cloud provider may intend to deceive the customer, and the customer must protect themselves

85. Which of the following is not typically included in an audit report?

    A. vendor list for remediations
    B. identified issues
    C. compliance determination
    D. risks

86. Audit management typically includes all of the following activities except _____.

    A. determining requirements
    B. scoping
    C. scheduling
    D. payment

87. Prospective cloud customers may have to submit _____ in order to gain access to audit reports.

    A. payment
    B. a surety bond
    C. a non-compete statement
    D. a non-disclosure agreement

88. If the customer wants to performer certain types of audits/assessments, they might require permission from the cloud provider. This is to distinguish the audit/assessment from _____.

    A. competitive influence

B. an attack ✓   p 58

C. an internal activity

D. normal customer operations

89. What is the term typically used to describe the documents, logs, and other materials used in an audit?

   A. stipulations

   B. data

   C. artifacts ✓

   D. ramifications

90. Compliance, audit, and assurance should be _____.

   A. entertaining

   B. expensive

   C. continuous ✓

   D. remote

91. _____ should evaluate the provider's third-party attestations and certifications, in order to align with compliance needs.

   A. regulators

   B. cloud providers

   C. cloud customers ✓

   D. end users

92. Cloud customers should consider using the _____ in order to track and maintain a record of cloud providers the customer uses, and record the providers' certification and compliance.

   A. National Institute for Standards and Technology (NIST) Special Publication (SP) 800-145, Cloud Computing Definition

B. The American Institute of Certified Public Accountants (AICPA) Statement of Standards for Attestation Engagements (SSAE) 18

C. the General Data Protection Regulation (GDPR)

✓ D. the Cloud Security Alliance (CSA) Cloud Controls Matrix (CCM)

p59

93. Cloud providers should engage in continuous compliance activities in order to avoid _____.

   A. additional financial penalties
   B. technological obsolescence
   C. creating compliance gaps ✓
   D. regulatory disapproval

94. Which of the following is a compliance artifact?

   A. a copy of the contract between the cloud customer and the provider
   B. a copy of administrative log data ✓
   C. a copy of the regulation used for oversight
   D. a copy of the law that creates the regulatory environment for a certain industry

95. Which of the following characteristics of cloud computing makes it unlikely that customers will be allowed to perform physical audits of cloud data centers?

   A. virtualization
   B. multitenancy ✓
   C. rapid elasticity
   D. metered service

96. Security practitioners aid the overall compliance effort of an organization

by _____.

    A. restricting physical access to the environment

    B. defeating external attackers

    C. evaluating and testing security controls ✓

    D. reviewing contracts from a security perspective

97. Which of the following probably has the most effect on compliance?

    A. jurisdictional differences ✓

    B. pricing models

    C. marketing behavior

    D. whether the cloud customer uses Windows, Apple, Linux/Unix, or another OS

98. What is the industry term for tools which are designed to aid in compliance assessment and reporting?

    A. DLP: data leak prevention

    ✓ B. GRC: governance, risk, and compliance

    C. DRM: digital rights management

    D. BCDR: business continuity and disaster recovery

99. Which of the following is not a standard requiring audit and compliance?

    A. the Payment Card Industry Data Security Standard (PCI-DSS)

    B. the Health Information Portability and Accountability Act (HIPAA)

    ✓ C. the X509 digital certificate standard

    D. the General Data Protect Regulation (GDPR)

100. Audit and assurance are included in an organization's _____.

    ✓ A. governance

B. profit margin

C. core competency

D. business continuity plan

DOMAIN 5
INFORMATION GOVERNANCE

CCSK Practice Tests – Cloud Security Alliance (CSA) Security Guidance v4

101. Which of the following is not one of the typical governance domains related to cloud computing?

     A. information classification

     B. pre-emptive litigation policies ✓

     C. information management policies

     D. location and jurisdiction policies

102. Which of the following is not one of the typical governance domains related to cloud computing?

     A. authorizations

     B. ownership

     C. fealty ✓

     D. privacy

103. Which of the following is not one of the typical governance domains related to cloud computing?

     A. contractual controls

     B. privacy

     C. security controls

D. ambiguity

104. Put the Phases of the Data Security Lifecycle in the proper order.

   A. Share
   B. Destroy
   C. Create
   D. Use
   E. Archive
   F. Store

   C
   F
   D
   A
   E
   B

105. Which of the following is not considered a typical Function in the Data Security Lifecycle?

   A. read
   B. write ✓
   C. process
   D. store

   p 65

106. Who is typically responsible for applying the proper security controls in the Create phase of the Data Security Lifecycle?

   A. the data subject
   B. regulators
   C. the data owner ✓
   D. the data processor

107. Which Phase of the Data Security Lifecycle occurs nearly simultaneously with the Create phase?

   A. Share
   B. Use
   C. Store ✓

D. Archive

108. The action of cryptoshredding probably takes place in the _____ phase of the Data Security Lifecycle.

   A. Create

   B. Share

   C. Archive

   D. Destroy ✓

109. Backups may be considered part of the _____ phase of the Data Security Lifecycle.

   A. Create

   B. Use

   C. Archive ✓

   D. Destroy

110. In order to extend organizational governance into the cloud, it is advised to use _____ and _____ controls. [select two]

   A. physical

   B. notional

   C. reprisal

   D. contractual ✓

   E. security ✓

   F. voluntary

   G. expensive

111. Before migrating to a cloud environment, the customer may have to _____.

   ✓ A. updating organizational policy to allow third-party management of data

B. secure funding from a lending institution

C. open the decision to a mandatory public comment period

D. request a cloud license from the ICANN (Internet Corporation for Assigned Names and Numbers)

112. Which of the following can be used to model data handling and controls?

    A. the CSA Cloud Controls Matrix (CCM)

    B. the Data Security Lifecycle

    C. the CSA Consensus Assessments Initiative Questionnaire (CAIQ)

    D. NIST (National Institute of Standards and Technology) Special Publication 800-37

113. Which of the following is not considered an "actor," according to the CSA Cloud Security Guidance v4?

    A. a person

    B. a device

    C. a system/process

    D. an application

114. An email may be considered part of the _____ phase of the Data Security Lifecycle.

    A. Create

    B. Store

    C. Share

    D. Use

115. Which of the following is true about the Data Security Lifecycle?

A. It is mandated for all cloud providers by the International Organization for Standardization (ISO

B. Not all data goes through all phases ✓   p63

C. US federal government agencies are required to use it, according to NIST regulations

D. It is strictly a contractual agreement

116. Which aspect of data governance extends an organization's requirements to a third party, such as a cloud provider?

    A. privacy

    B. nonrepudiation

    C. contractual controls ✓

    D. enhancement

117. Who is the data owner, in a cloud computing relationship?

    A. the cloud customer ✓

    B. the cloud provider

    C. the auditor

    D. the data subject

118. Which organizational entity is probably most suited for understand jurisdictional compliance requirements?

    A. the security office

    B. the information technology (IT) department

    C. senior management

    D. the legal department ✓

119. Information governance includes the _____ and _____ used to ensure data is handled in accordance to organizational controls and requirements. [select two]

A. vendors

B. security controls ✓

C. corporate structures ✓ p60

D. licensing fees

E. impartial observers

F. reasonable person

120. According to the CSA Cloud Security Guidance v4, what is the definition of information/data governance?

   A. applying the highest possible degree of security to an environment

   ✓ B. ensuring the use of data and information complies with organizational policies, standards and strategy—including regulatory, contractual, and business objectives

   C. providing the greatest customer care

   D. complying the absolute most regulatory and legal requirements across the greatest number of jurisdictions

   p 60

DOMAIN 6
MANAGEMENT PLANE AND BUSINESS CONTINUITY

CCSK Practice Tests - Cloud Security Alliance (CSA) Security Guidance v4

121. According to the CSA Cloud Security Guidance v4, what is the single most significant security difference between cloud computing and traditional IT infrastructure?

    A. virtualization

    B. microprocessors

    C. the user community

    D. the management plane ✓

122. As an analogy, gaining access to the management plane is like _____.

    A. getting access to all personnel records

    B. getting physical access to your building

    C. getting access to all traffic entering and leaving your IT environment

    D. getting unfettered access to your data center ✓

123. Who is responsible for securing and managing the credentials used to access the management plane?

A. the cloud provider

B. the cloud customer ✓

C. regulators

D. the user

124. Which of the following is not a main aspect of business continuity/disaster recovery (BCDR) in the cloud?

A. considering options for portability

B. preparing for and managing provider outages

C. ensuring continuity and recovery within a given cloud provider

✗ D. lobbying legislators to create legal constraints for cloud providers

125. _____ is a cloud business continuity/disaster recovery (BCDR) feature that is not easily accomplished in a traditional (on-prem) IT environment.

A. regular backups

✓ B. deploying virtual machines across multiple, distinct geographic availability zones

C. versioning of baseline operating system (OS) builds

D. personnel training

126. In which service model is the customer more likely to have the ability to architect the cloud environment for resiliency?

A. IaaS ✓

B. PaaS

C. SaaS

D. public

127. Which of the following are essential for a risk-based approach to

business continuity/disaster recovery (BCDR) in the cloud? [select all that apply]

- ✓ A. not all assets need equal continuity
- ✓ B. you don't need to plan for full provider outages; review the historical performance of the provider
- ✓ C. try to design your environment to meet the same goals (recovery time objective [RTO] and recovery point objective [RPO]) you used for your traditional environment
- D. always purchase the highest-cost provider package, to ensure the utmost availability

128. What sort of interface does the cloud customer typically have with the management plane in an SaaS cloud model?

- A. root-level access of the underlying hardware
- ✓ B. an "admin" tab on the user panel
- C. administrative access to the operating system the app runs on
- D. physical access to the data center itself

129. The management plane is instrumental for enabling and enforcing _____ and _____ in multitenancy. [select two]

- A. refraction
- B. implementation
- C. isolation ✓
- D. separation ✓
- E. navigation
- F. compensation

130. The management plane includes the interfaces for _____ and also the interfaces for _____. [select two]

- A. building and managing the cloud itself ✓

B. allowing auditors access to inspect the environment

C. permitting regulators to review the cloud architecture

D. end users to enter the physical data center

E. government agents to surveil web traffic

F. cloud customers to manage their own allocated resources in the cloud

131. What are the two typical ways cloud providers deliver management plane access to customers? [select two]

A. overnight shipping

B. web consoles

C. APIs

D. add-ins to operating systems (OSs)

E. portable media

132. Web consoles for accessing the cloud management plane are managed by the _____.

A. cloud provider

B. cloud customer

C. regulator

D. programmer

133. The web console's _____ might be customized to a particular customer's organization, to create that organization's own "version" of the console.

A. color scheme

B. logo

C. domain name

D. preferred browser

134. Cloud management plane APIs are typically created with _____.

   A. care
   B. representational state transfer (REST) ✓
   C. simple object access protocol (SOAP)
   D. extensible markup language (XML)

135. REST APIs run over _____, and therefore work well across diverse environments.

   A. fiber lines
   B. all obstacles
   C. wifi
   D. HTTP/S ✓

136. REST API authentication commonly uses _____ or _____. [select two]

   A. ticket-granting tickets (TGT)
   B. HTTP request signing
   C. quad processors
   D. OAuth ✓
   E. large fonts

137. Identity and access (IAM) typically includes all of the following except _____.

   A. identification
   B. isolation ✗
   C. authentication
   D. authorization

138. The cloud customer's root account, which can be used to create or

destroy the entire configuration, should have all the following qualities except _____.

A. enterprise-owned

B. almost never used

C. secured

D. easy to recover ✓ p 70

139. All privileged accounts should use _____.

A. extensible markup language (XML)

✓ B. multifactor authentication

C. alphanumeric passphrases with special characters

D. 16 character-credentials

140. _____ is one of the single most effective security controls to defend against a wide variety of attacks.

A. A firewall

B. Infrared camera surveillance   p 71

C. Egress monitoring

✓ D. Multifactor authentication

141. Virtualizing resources into pools typically creates an environment where resiliency is decreased for _____.

A. any single virtual asset/machine ✓

B. international customers   p 73

C. fiber networks

D. ISO-certified systems

142. _____ allows the cloud customer to create an infrastructure template to configure all or some aspects of a cloud deployment.

A. REST APIs

B. artificial intelligence (AI)

C. intrinsic motivation

D. software-defined infrastructure (SDI)

143. What is probably the most significant barrier to implementing cloud business continuity/disaster recovery (BCDR) architecture across multiple geographic locations?

   A. cost

   B. legal prohibitions

   C. loss of users

   D. nonrepeatability of the web console's color scheme

144. What is the term used to describe a security methodology that tests the overall resilience of the environment by selectively disabling components?

   A. inventive pragmatism

   B. structural adherence

   C. plaintive wailing

   D. chaos engineering

145. Prepare for _____ in case of a provider outage.

   A. bankruptcy

   B. graceful failure

   C. cataclysmic results

   D. legal repercussions

DOMAIN 7
INFRASTRUCTURE SECURITY

CCSK Practice Tests - Cloud Security Alliance (CSA) Security Guidance v4

146. For cloud providers, there are typically three different physical networks in a data center. Which of these is not one of the typical networks?

    A. service

    B. storage

    C. management

    D. review

147. What are the two general categories of network virtualization common in cloud environments? [select two]

    A. perforated

    B. VLAN (virtual local area network)

    C. SaaS

    D. hypervisor

    E. SDN (software-defined networking)

    F. TPS (total processing simulation)

148. Software-defined networks (SDNs) decouple the control plane from the _____.

A. data plane

B. data center

C. customer

D. Internet

149. Software-defined networks (SDNs) offer higher _____ and _____. [select two]

A. risk

B. cost

C. abridgement

D. flexibility

E. isolation

F. regulation

150. Software-defined networks (SDNs) offer _____, allowing customers to extend existing networks into the cloud.

A. proprietary data formats

B. software definition of IP ranges

C. a homogenous hardware approach

D. limited interactivity with other networks

151. Software-defined networks often use _____ so that virtual machines and other assets do not require modification to the underlying network stack to communicate with each other.

A. alternating current (AC)

B. data leak protection (DLP) solutions

C. packet encapsulation

D. rarified prohibition

152. Perhaps the most significant difference between the traditional and cloud environments that will affect security.

   A. connecting the customer's network to the outside world (including the Internet)

   B. the requirement of hardware to interact with software

   C. the requirement of hardware to connect to other hardware elements

   D. lack of customer access to the underlying physical hardware/network

153. The use of virtual security appliances in a cloud environment may cause _____ because they must intercept all network traffic.

   A. intermittent outages

   B. end-user dissatisfaction

   C. traffic slowdown

   D. cost fluctuation

154. The use of virtual appliances for security in the cloud environment might negatively affect elasticity because product vendors might not support auto-scaling of _____.

   A. appliance traffic

   B. new product instances

   C. additional users

   D. licensing

155. Virtual appliances used for security in a cloud environment should monitor cloud assets according to _____.

   A. IP address

   B. network name

   C. unique ID

D. region

156. The use of firewalls in software-defined networks (SDNs), often referred to as "security groups," allow for _____ control of traffic and access control.

    A. simple

    B. granular

    C. expensive

    D. immediate

157. Unlike physical network security appliances, firewalls in software-defined networking (SDN) are typically _____.

    A. free of charge

    B. set to default-deny

    C. not effective

    D. broad in effect

158. One of the benefits of microsegmentation is that each _____ can exist on its own network.

    A. data center

    B. application

    C. user

    D. organization

159. Having assets on separate networks promotes security by _____.

    A. putting an extra layer of access control on data files

    B. blocking external distributed denial of service (DDOS) attacks

    C. protecting data from privileged account holders

    D. reducing the potential impact if an attacker gets access to an asset

160. The use and implementation of microsegmentation may increase _____.

    A. capital expenses

    B. enterprise risk

    C. regulatory oversight

    D. operational expenses

161. Which of the following is not part of the software-defined perimeter (SDP) model, defined by the CSA SDP Working Group?

    A. an asset that connects to the cloud

    B. an SDP motivator

    C. an SDP controller

    D. an SDP gateway

162. Which of the following is not a recommended tool for enforcing separation between private and public clouds in a hybrid cloud deployment?

    A. firewalls

    B. digital rights management (DRM)

    C. routing

    D. access controls

163. Which of the following is not one of the challenges created by hybrid cloud deployments?

    A. increased routing complexity

    B. additional costs for registering domain names

    C. reduces the ability to run multiple cloud networks with overlapping IP ranges

D. complicates security because of the need to harmonize controls

164. How does a "bastion" or "transit" virtual network architecture assist in a hybrid cloud deployment?

   A. the second-level networks are not peered to each other, and therefore effectively segregated

   B. users are kept from accessing the public cloud, reducing overall risk

   C. throttling of traffic eliminates the possibility of denial of service (DOS/DDOS) attacks

   D. authentication of each service is increased in general

165. Which of the following might be considered a cloud "workload"? [Select all that apply.]

   A. an element of credit card data

   B. an individual user

   C. a virtual machine

   D. a private business

   E. a container

   F. a nation-state

166. Workloads always _____ and _____ [select two]

   A. run on a processor

   B. consume memory

   C. cross international borders

   D. cause user error

167. One reason containers can launch quickly.

   A. they are always loaded from solid-state drives (SSDs)

B. they do not have to boot operating systems (OSs)

C. they have neutrino memory

D. there are very many of them in the public cloud

168. Who is responsible for creating and enforcing segregation in the hardware stack of cloud computing?

    A. the user

    B. the cloud customer

    C. the cloud provider

    D. regulators

169. One of the characteristics of immutable workloads.

    A. no need to patch individual virtual machines

    B. users cannot make any errors

    C. legal in all jurisdictions

    D. immune to malware

170. _____ is essential to proper management of an immutable environment.

    A. consistency in the image creation process

    B. highly-paid engineers

    C. the proper geophysical location

    D. auditor approval

DOMAIN 8
VIRTUALIZATION AND CONTAINERS

CCSK Practice Tests - Cloud Security Alliance (CSA) Security Guidance v4

171. What is the main reason process isolation in a cloud environment is so important?

    A. regulatory requirement

    B. cost

    C. multitenancy

    D. efficiency

172. All of the following are typical security controls available to cloud customers except _____.

    A. monitoring and logging

    B. cloud provider personnel reviews

    C. image asset management

    D. use of dedicated hosting

173. Which of the following is not considered a major virtualization category, according to the Cloud Security Alliance?

    A. compute

    B. networking

    C. user

    D. storage

174. One of the reasons software-defined networking (SDN) may be preferable to virtual local area networks (VLANs) in the cloud.

A. VLANs are more expensive

B. VLANs are not approved by regulators

C. VLANs may not provide sufficient isolation

D. VLANs are not as fast as SDNs

175. A reason that traditional network monitoring devices deployed in a cloud environment may not work effectively.

A. communication between virtual machines on the same hardware device might not be routed through any physical network

B. auditors cannot review virtual images

C. regulators might insist that a certain process be hosted in a traditional environment

D. certain jurisdictions may outlaw this practice

176. Instead of using physical firewall appliances, which may not be as effective in the cloud environment, cloud customers may opt for using _____ to achieve the same purpose.

A. strong contract terms

B. the firewall solution(s) offered by the provider

C. digital rights management (DRM)

D. user training

177. Which of the following could be considered the top security priority for cloud providers?

A. protecting their own intellectual property

B. segregating and isolating customer traffic

C. providing maximum bandwidth

D. designing application programming interfaces (APIs) that optimize customers' business goals

178. A special kind of wide area network (WAN) virtualization technology used to span multiple "base" networks.

A. virtual local area network (VLAN)

B. Wifi

C. overlay network

D. maximal networking

179. Two common forms of storage virtualization in traditional (on-prem) IT environments. [select two]

   A. hypertext transfer protocol (HTTP)

   B. virtual local area network (VLAN)

   C. storage-area network (SAN)

   D. Hippo

   E. Apache

   F. network-attached storage (NAS)

180. What method is commonly used to ensure that swapping out a storage drive won't inadvertently reveal data?

   A. watermarking

   B. encryption

   C. superimposition

   D. steganography

181. Which of the following is a highly portable code execution environment?

   A. container

   B. web server

   C. Kerberos

   D. OAuth

182. Containers typically provide runtime environments that share a common _____.

   A. vernacular

   B. operating system (OS)

   C. molecular bond

   D. kernel

183. If data is encrypted at the virtual layer, the data may not be protected from exposure to _____.

   A. users
   B. external attackers
   C. the cloud provider
   D. regulators

184. Which of the following is not a component of typical software container systems?

   A. the execution environment
   B. a GUI interface for user interaction
   C. an orchestration and scheduling controller
   D. a repository for the container images or code to execute

185. Which of the following is not a required security measure for containers, regardless of the type of container?

   A. physical security of the underlying hardware
   B. securing the management plane
   C. properly securing the image repository
   D. encrypting the code of the container as it runs

186. Container solutions should, at a minimum, support role-based access controls and _____, for security purposes.

   A. strong authentication
   B. biometric physical security
   C. personnel background checks
   D. elliptic-curve encryption

187. In-depth understanding of container solutions is predicated on a thorough understanding of _____.

   A. security fundamentals
   B. policy promulgation
   C. operating system internals

D. encryption methodologies

188. Which of the following is not an element of the operating system?

    A. namespaces

    B. divestiture

    C. memory

    D. network port mapping

189. Whose responsibility is it to implement virtualization features with a secure-by-default configuration?

    A. the cloud customer

    B. the regulator

    C. the cloud provider

    D. the auditor

190. Whose responsibility is it to configure hypervisors to isolate virtual machines from each other?

    A. the cloud customer

    B. the regulator

    C. the cloud provider

    D. the auditor

191. Whose responsibility is it to group containers of the same security context on the same physical and/or virtual hosts?

    A. the cloud customer

    B. the regulator

    C. the cloud provider

    D. the auditor

192. Whose responsibility is it to implement appropriate role-based access controls and strong authentication for all container and repository management?

    A. the cloud customer

    B. the regulator

C. the cloud provider

D. the auditor

193. Whose responsibility is it to determine compliance with a given standard/regulation, from an objective perspective?

    A. the cloud customer

    B. the regulator

    C. the cloud provider

    D. the auditor

194. Which of the following is not a crucial security responsibility typically expected of the cloud provider?

    A. use secure hypervisors and implement a patch management process to keep them up to date

    B. secure the credentials used by customers to access the management plane

    C. configure hypervisors to isolate virtual machines from each other

    D. implement processes to prevent administrative access to running virtual machines or volatile memory

195. In order to reduce the possibility that administrators working for the cloud provider get access to customer data, the cloud provider should _____.

    A. isolate encryption services from data-management functions

    B. ensure all cloud customer employees are trained in the most current security tools

    C. make digital rights management (DRM) solutions available to customers

    D. ensure that only approved, known, secure container images or code can be deployed

DOMAIN 9
INCIDENT RESPONSE

CCSK Practice Tests - Cloud Security Alliance (CSA) Security Guidance v4

196. The CSA Guidance uses which standard for describing the incident response process?

    A. ISO 27035

    B. ENISA strategies for incident response

    C. ANSI 5756

    D. NIST SP 800-61

197. Which of the following is not a phase of the incident response process described in the CSA Guidance?

    A. preparation

    B. isolation

    C. detection and analysis

    D. post-mortem

198. Which of the following activities should occur in the Preparation phase of the incident response lifecycle?

    A. build a timeline of the attack

    B. take systems offline

    C. determine the extent of data loss

D. subscribing to third-party threat intelligence services

199. Which phase of the incident response lifecycle is used to determine ways to improve the incident response process?

    A. preparation

    B. detection and analysis

    C. containment, eradication, and recovery

    D. post-mortem

200. Which phase of the incident response lifecycle is affected by migrating from a traditional IT environment to the cloud?

    A. preparation

    B. isolation

    C. post-mortem

    D. all of them

201. Which of the following is not a recommendation from the CSA about cloud customer incident response activity during the Preparation phase?

    A. test the incident response notification process

    B. the provider and customer should engage in joint training sessions involving personnel from both organizations

    C. ensure the provider has accurate notification contact information for the customer

    D. the customer should ensure they have correct notification/escalation contact information for the provider

202. In preparing for incident response for an IaaS/PaaS environment, the cloud customer should be aware...

    A. of which hardware elements comprise the underlying infrastructure

- B. that log data for a specific incident might be limited to what was already provided according to the contract
- C. of any users logging into the environment remotely
- D. of the time delay from the moment of incident detection until the arrival of armed response

203. A customer should design the cloud environment in a way that optimizes the effectiveness of incident response. This includes all of the following measures except _____.

- A. enable API logging to an external, secure location
- B. ensure contracts include a 100% uptime guarantee
- C. utilize isolation to limit potential negative impact
- D. use immutable servers if possible

204. Which of the following are helpful ways to determine if your architecture is suitable for incident containment? [select all that apply]

- A. conduct user training at periodic intervals
- B. threat modeling activities
- C. tabletop exercises
- D. ensure cloud provider billing is accurate
- E. protect root management credentials

205. If logs aren't available to determine possible changes/modifications in the cloud environment, what might the customer use instead (depending on which provider the customer is using)?

- A. forensic hardware
- B. the cloud management console
- C. digital rights management software
- D. strong contract language

206. To aid in getting information about potential attackers, the cloud customer might consider _____.

    A. subscribing to an external threat intelligence service

    B. sending undercover operatives into known attacker hangouts

    C. paying known attackers for insight into their operations

    D. offering a bounty to anyone who will attack the attackers

207. In order to determine whether log data received from a cloud provider satisfies chain-of-custody requirements, security practitioners should consult _____.

    A. their supervisors

    B. senior management

    C. attorneys

    D. cloud providers

208. Because of the dynamic and high-velocity nature of cloud environments, it is best to _____ forensic/investigatory processes.

    A. remove

    B. replicate

    C. reduce

    D. automate

209. Processes that might be automated in order to enhance incident response actions in the cloud include all of the following except _____.

    A. snapshotting the storage of a virtual machine

    B. capturing metadata at the time of an alert

    C. reviewing alerts to determine their precedence

    D. "pausing" a virtual machine, to retain volatile memory (if allowed by the provider)

210. Cloud capabilities that might assist with determining the extent of the impact of an incident include: [select all that apply]

   A. analyze network flows to determine if isolation was compromised

   B. metered service

   C. virtualization

   D. examine configuration data to see if similar instances were exposed in the same attack

   E. query intelligence-sharing centers for the industry

211. What part of the incident containment procedure should be conducted first?

   A. shut down affected machines (real or virtual)

   B. determine if an attacker has access to the management console

   C. rewrite damaged data

   D. terminate guilty personnel

212. If the cloud customer suspects the management plane has been breached, the customer should be sure to _____.

   A. notify law enforcement

   B. notify shareholders

   C. contract with external auditors

   D. confirm that templates for new workloads have not been compromised

213. During the post-mortem phase of the incident response process, the cloud customer may want to _____ the Service Level Agreement (SLA).

   A. terminate

   B. violate

C. adopt

D. renegotiate

214. In the cloud, the use of _____ and _____ monitoring capabilities may offer incident detection earlier than similar efforts in the traditional IT environment. [select two]

    A. oblique

    B. inferred

    C. continuous

    D. serverless

    E. sentient

215. Data sources (such as logs) used in the incident response process should be handled in a way that _____.

    A. indicts the criminals

    B. terminates employees

    C. severs unauthorized connections

    D. preserves the chain of custody

DOMAIN 10
APPLICATION SECURITY

CCSK Practice Tests - Cloud Security Alliance (CSA) Security Guidance v4

216. Which incentive drives cloud providers to create higher baseline security for the application environment than a traditional environment?

    A. celebratory

    B. financial

    C. emotional

    D. honor

217. A security opportunity that may make the cloud computing environment advantageous compared to the traditional IT environment.

    A. responsiveness

    B. physical centralization

    C. single point of failure

    D. hardware homogeneity

218. A security opportunity that may make the cloud computing environment advantageous compared to the traditional IT environment.

    A. cross-jurisdictional

    B. isolated environments

    C. single set of credentials

D. impenetrable physical security

219. A security opportunity that may make the cloud computing environment advantageous compared to the traditional IT environment.

    A. regulatory capture

    B. corporate financing

    C. independent virtual machines

    D. Internet connectivity

220. A security opportunity that may make the cloud computing environment advantageous compared to the traditional IT environment.

    A. elasticity

    B. remote access

    C. shared responsibilities

    D. coercion

221. A security opportunity that may make the cloud computing environment advantageous compared to the traditional IT environment.

    A. waterfall

    B. spiral

    C. angle

    D. DevOps

222. A security opportunity that may make the cloud computing environment advantageous compared to the traditional IT environment.

    A. reverse identity

    B. unified interface

    C. shared responsibilities

    D. provider administration

223. A security challenge that may make the cloud computing environment risky compared to the traditional IT environment.

   A. the use of software

   B. limited detailed visibility

   C. users

   D. physical security

224. A security challenge that may make the cloud computing environment risky compared to the traditional IT environment.

   A. increased application scope

   B. increased price of services

   C. lack of processing power

   D. limited number of providers

225. A security challenge that may make the cloud computing environment risky compared to the traditional IT environment.

   A. arbitrary enforcement

   B. binary data

   C. changing threat models

   D. deletion of files

226. A security challenge that may make the cloud computing environment risky compared to the traditional IT environment.

   A. reduced price

   B. reduced remote access capability

   C. reduced storage capacity

   D. reduced transparency

227. Which of the following is not one of the CSA's "meta-phases" used to

describe the secure software development lifecycle (SSDLC) for the cloud environment?

    A. secure design and development

    B. secure testing

    C. secure deployment

    D. secure operations

228. Cloud computing affects _____ phase(s) of the secure software development lifecycle (SSDLC).

    A. many

    B. one

    C. the secure operations

    D. all

229. One of the reasons cloud computing affects the secure software development lifecycle (SSDLC).

    A. the shared responsibilities model

    B. cloud entails operational expenditures instead of capital expenditures

    C. regulatory mandates

    D. only one SSDLC framework exists for cloud software development

230. Every cloud provider has _____ capabilities in terms of features, security, and security, which may affect the secure software development lifecycle (SSDLC).

    A. the same

    B. compliant

    C. different

    D. perfect

231. Applying the secure software development lifecycle (SSDLC) in the cloud may differ from using it in the traditional IT environment because _____ might be included in the scope of application security.

    A. users

    B. external mandates

    C. price

    D. the management plane

232. Which of the following is not an organizational department that will need new, specific training to learn how to handle the secure software development lifecycle (SSDLC) in the cloud environment when the organization migrates from the traditional environment?

    A. development

    B. operations

    C. security

    D. regulatory

233. In which step of the secure software development (SSDLC) process should the deployment process(es) first be determined?

    A. deploy

    B. design

    C. define

    D. test

234. In which step of the secure software development (SSDLC) process should threat modeling be applied?

    A. define

    B. develop

    C. destroy

    D. design

235. The development environment should never contain _____.

    A. management plane access to the cloud environment

    B. developers

    C. virtual machines

    D. production data

236. What tool might be used to compensate for the lack of network, system, or service logs in a PaaS cloud application development environment?

    A. security incident and event management (SIEM) solutions

    B. application logs

    C. digital rights management (DRM)

    D. data loss prevention (DLP) solutions

237. Cloud customers engaged in application development for a cloud environment should rely more on _____ testing.

    A. manual

    B. vendor-based

    C. physical

    D. automated

238. One form of manual testing that might be very useful in cloud application development.

    A. vulnerability scans

    B. fuzz testing

    C. code review

    D. pressure tests

239. Benefits of using a continuous integration/continuous deployment

(CI/CD) pipeline model of cloud application development include: [select all that apply]

    A. reduce costs

    B. enhance market acceptance

    C. capture increased market share

    D. support immutable infrastructure

    E. automate security testing

    F. offer opportunity to log application and infrastructure changes

240. A security benefit of using the DevOps approach to application development in the cloud.

    A. standardizing the development, testing, and operational environments

    B. reducing overall costs for the organization

    C. removing user input from the development process

    D. guaranteeing approval of all audits

DOMAIN 11
DATA SECURITY AND ENCRYPTION

CCSK Practice Tests - Cloud Security Alliance (CSA) Security Guidance v4

241. Which of the following is a crucial control for protecting and managing data in the cloud environment? [select all that apply]

    A. architecture

    B. encryption

    C. access controls

    D. monitoring/alerting

    E. additional controls, such as data loss prevention (DLP)

242. Which of the following is not a category of data security controls discussed in the CSA Cloud Security Guidance v4, Domain 11?

    A. controlling which data goes into the cloud

    B. protecting and managing data in the cloud

    C. enforcing information lifecycle management

    D. training users who access the cloud environment

243. Which of the following are main data storage types in the cloud? [select all that apply]

    A. object

    B. volume

C. translucent

D. database

244. A redundant, durable data storage mechanism used in the cloud.

　　A. ephemeral

　　B. epiphany

　　C. data dispersion

　　D. RAM

245. Also known as a Cloud Security Gateway, this solution helps your organization determine how your users are consuming cloud services.

　　A. firewalls

　　B. security incident and event monitoring systems (SIEMs)

　　C. application programming interfaces (APIs)

　　D. cloud access security brokers (CASBs)

246. Basically, a virtual hard drive for instances/virtual machines.

　　A. object storage

　　B. volume storage

　　C. content delivery network (CDN)

　　D. software-defined networking (SDN)

247. Managing which data goes into the cloud is the responsibility of the _____.

　　A. regulator

　　B. provider

　　C. customer

　　D. administrator

248. Managing which data is put into the cloud is often as important, or more important, for _____ purposes than for security purposes.

   A. financial

   B. aesthetic

   C. training

   D. compliance

249. A data loss prevention (DLP) solution might not work properly if data is _____.

   A. stored as plaintext

   B. sent via email

   C. encrypted

   D. stored on magnetic media

250. For migrating data to the cloud, the most secure of the following options is _____.

   A. email the data to a virtual machine in the cloud

   B. set up a secure file transfer protocol (SFTP) server in the cloud

   C. send the provider a flashstick via the postal service

   D. use the provider's proprietary application programming interface (API)

251. _____ is an essential security capability; if a provider does not offer this function, do not use that provider.

   A. training and awareness of the customer

   B. transport layer security (TLS)

   C. secure sockets layer (SSL)

   D. digital rights management (DRM)

252. If your organization must accept untrusted data into its cloud environment (such as public input), it is important to _____ the data first.

   A. isolate and scan

   B. encrypt

   C. hash

   D. save

253. According to the CSA Cloud Security Guidance v4, _____ and encryption are the core data security elements in the cloud.

   A. training

   B. physical controls

   C. access controls

   D. digital rights management (DRM)

254. Access controls in the cloud should be implemented with a minimum of three layers in order to provide data security. Which of the following is not one of those layers?

   A. management plane

   B. public and internal sharing controls

   C. physical controls

   D. application level controls

255. Most cloud providers use a default _____ policy for management plane access control.

   A. deny

   B. delete

   C. allow

   D. overwrite

256. Where possible, the customer should use a(n) _____ encryption key.

   A. advanced encryption standard (AES)

   B. symmetric

   C. one-way

   D. customer-managed

257. The cloud customer should not rely entirely on encryption and access controls for data security but should also consider _____.

   A. user training

   B. secure architecture

   C. inverse proportions

   D. physical mechanisms

258. _____ should not be included in the test environment.

   A. code under development

   B. new systems

   C. security

   D. raw production data

259. Digitals rights management (DRM) solutions are tools used to secure data by placing additional access control on specific files; unfortunately, DRM relies on _____, so use of DRM may reduce certain functionality offered by cloud providers.

   A. user awareness

   B. encryption

   C. creativity

   D. administrative rights

260. Data loss prevention (DLP) solutions are not typically deployed in _____, so it works better in SaaS than PaaS or IaaS.

    A. remote locations

    B. the cloud

    C. commercial websites

    D. data centers

261. Logs from monitoring solutions should be stored in _____.

    A. the cloud

    B. a secure location

    C. an on-prem storage option

    D. underground bunkers

262. When the cloud provider manages cryptographic keys, the key storage and production environments are generally separate, reducing the possibility keys are exposed. However, keys might still be exposed by _____.

    A. user error

    B. misconfiguration

    C. governmental request

    D. failure of the physical infrastructure

263. Which of the following is not a typical option for managing encryption keys in the cloud?

    A. hardware security module (HSM)/appliance

    B. virtual appliance/software

    C. cloud provider service

    D. regulator storage

264. Which of the following is not one of the main considerations of key management in the cloud?

   A. performance

   B. latency

   C. security

   D. visibility

265. When data is stored as objects in the back-end of an application, the encryption engine for encrypting the data should be located in the application or _____.

   A. cloud

   B. physical device

   C. client

   D. portable device

DOMAIN 12
IDENTITY, ENTITLEMENT AND ACCESS MANAGEMENT

CCSK Practice Tests - Cloud Security Alliance (CSA) Security Guidance v4

266. Which party solely manages the identity and access management (IAM) responsibilities in the cloud?

    A. the cloud provider

    B. no single party

    C. the cloud customer

    D. the regulator

267. Which of the following is not a crucial component of the identity and access management relationship between customer and provider?

    A. trust relationships

    B. legal framework

    C. designation of responsibilities

    D. technical mechanics of implementation

268. The primary tool used to provision identities across multiple cloud platforms/services/systems.

    A. digital rights management (DRM)

    B. data loss prevention (DLP)

C. federation

D. virtualization

269. The process/mechanism used to confirm that an identity assertion belongs to the entity presenting it.

    A. identification

    B. authentication

    C. authorization

    D. auditing

270. A common authentication factor.

    A. the CCSK certification

    B. gainful employment

    C. security clearance

    D. password

271. An identity assertion must be _____.

    A. confidential

    B. shared

    C. neglected

    D. unique

272. An XML-based OASIS federation standard.

    A. SAML (Security Assertion Markup Language)

    B. CANT (Coordinated Access Networking Topology)

    C. Linux

    D. REST (REpresentational State Transfer)

273. Which of the following is not an element of SAML?

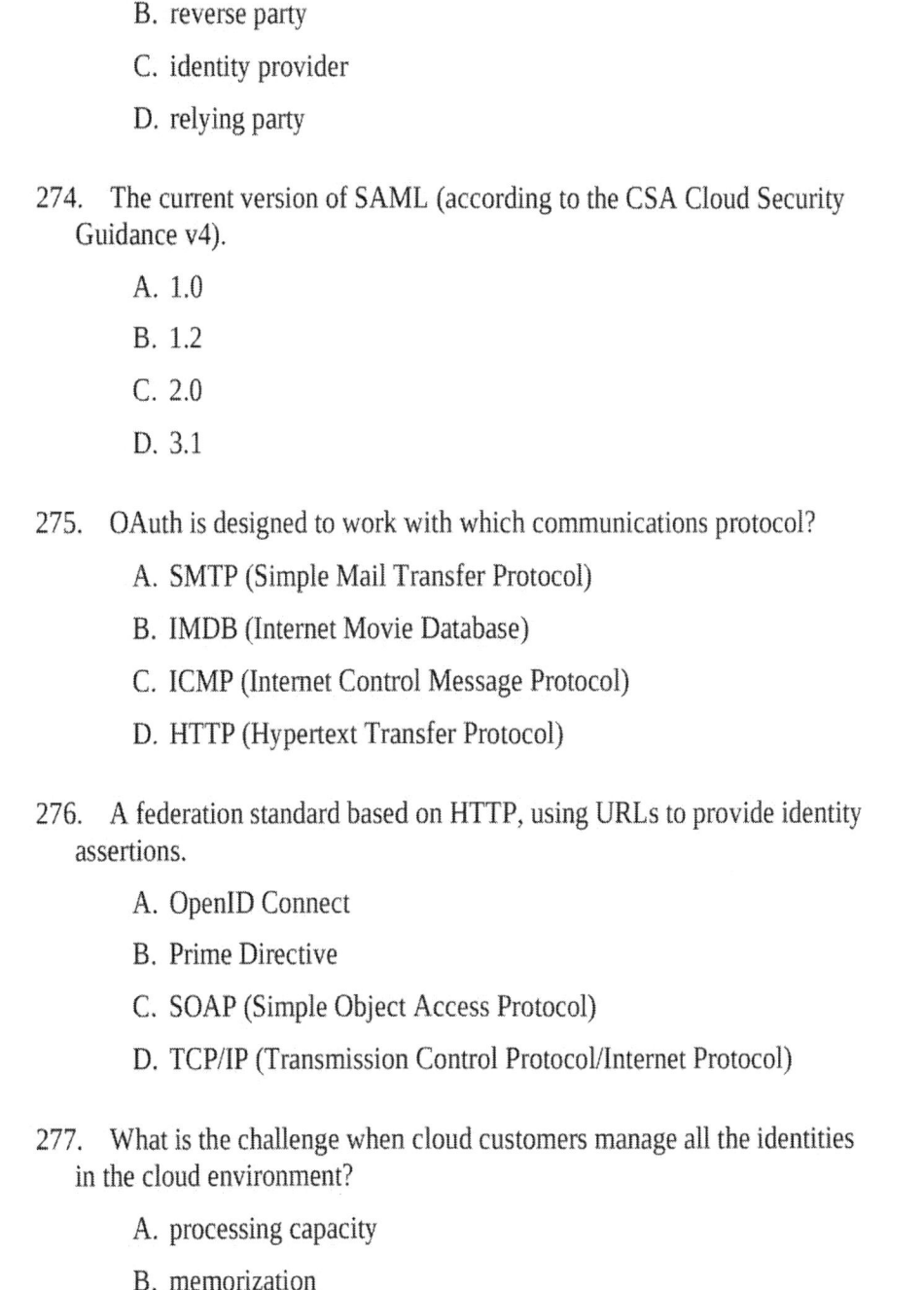

A. identity assertions

B. reverse party

C. identity provider

D. relying party

274. The current version of SAML (according to the CSA Cloud Security Guidance v4).

    A. 1.0

    B. 1.2

    C. 2.0

    D. 3.1

275. OAuth is designed to work with which communications protocol?

    A. SMTP (Simple Mail Transfer Protocol)

    B. IMDB (Internet Movie Database)

    C. ICMP (Internet Control Message Protocol)

    D. HTTP (Hypertext Transfer Protocol)

276. A federation standard based on HTTP, using URLs to provide identity assertions.

    A. OpenID Connect

    B. Prime Directive

    C. SOAP (Simple Object Access Protocol)

    D. TCP/IP (Transmission Control Protocol/Internet Protocol)

277. What is the challenge when cloud customers manage all the identities in the cloud environment?

    A. processing capacity

    B. memorization

C. storage capacity

D. scalability

278. Cloud computing affects the way identity and access management (IAM) is handled, in ways that are quite different than the traditional IT environment. According to the CSA Cloud Security Guidance v4, the biggest impact cloud has on IAM is a greater need for _____ and _____. [select two]

   A. user training

   B. threat intelligence

   C. strong authentication

   D. the use of multiple authentication factors

   E. deployment of hardware tokens

   F. reliance on biometric authentication

279. A tool used to map out access rights and permissions against authenticated identity assertions and characteristics.

   A. attribute portal

   B. entitlement matrix

   C. facet corollary

   D. digital rights management (DRM)

280. The _____ is responsible for enforcing access controls and authorizations.

   A. cloud customer

   B. cloud provider

   C. regulator

   D. user

DOMAIN 13
SECURITY AS A SERVICE

CCSK Practice Tests - Cloud Security Alliance (CSA) Security Guidance v4

281. In order to be considered security-as-a-service (SecaaS) according to the Cloud Security Alliance (CSA), the technology must _____.

    A. reside entirely within one jurisdiction

    B. serve cloud environments

    C. be certified according to the CSA Security, Trust, Assurance, and Risk (STAR) Registry Level 3

    D. be delivered as a cloud service

282. In order to be considered security-as-a-service (SecaaS) according to the Cloud Security Alliance (CSA), the technology must _____.

    A. meet the NIST definition of a cloud service

    B. be accessed via virtual private networks (VPNs)

    C. use transport layer security (TLS)

    D. satisfy GDPR (General Data Protection Regulation) requirements

283. All of the following are potential benefits of security-as-a-service (SecaaS), except _____. [choose all that apply]

    A. reduced capital investment

    B. data leakage

    C. expertise

D. intelligence-sharing

E. insulation of clients

284. All of the following are potential benefits of security-as-a-service (SecaaS), except _____ . [choose all that apply].

   A. scaling

   B. cost

   C. cloud-computing benefits

   D. changing providers

   E. migration

285. Why might security-as-a-service (SecaaS) providers have difficulty meeting the regulatory requirements of potential customers?

   A. cloud is global

   B. customers won't pay for it

   C. providers are uneducated

   D. regulators hate the cloud

286. Which term describes a cloud security gateway?

   A. the Security, Trust, Assurance, and Risk (STAR) Registry

   B. a Cloud Access Security Broker (CASB)

   C. the Cloud Controls Matrix (CCM)

   D. the General Data Protection Regualtion (GDPR)

287. _____ is one type of security-as-a-service (SecaaS).

   A. transparent encryption

   B. Type 2 hypervisor

   C. federated identity brokers

   D. remote meetings

288. Security-as-a-service (SecaaS) providers might offer strong authentication capabilities, such as mobile device applications and _____.

   A. user training and awareness
   B. AES encryption
   C. flotation devices
   D. tokens for multifactor authentication

289. Cloud-based security-as-a-service (SecaaS) offerings for web security gateways might include both proxy capabilities and _____.

   A. redirecting web traffic
   B. deep packet inspection
   C. heuristic algorithms
   D. the Turing test

290. Security-as-a-service providers might offer all the following types of solutions except _____. [select all that apply]

   A. security management
   B. financial oversight
   C. business continuity and disaster recovery (BCDR)
   D. distributed denial of service (DDOS) protection
   E. legal advice
   F. encryption and key management

DOMAIN 14
RELATED TECHNOLOGIES

CCSK Practice Tests - Cloud Security Alliance (CSA) Security Guidance v4

291. Which of the following is not one of the common components of "big data" solutions?

    A. distributed data collection

    B. distributed billing

    C. distributed storage

    D. distributed processing

292. Which of the following is not one of the security risks often associated with "Internet of Things (IoT)"?

    A. weak or outdated encryption schemes

    B. application programming interface (API) vulnerabilities

    C. data collection and sanitization

    D. severe opportunity for human error

293. Which of the following is a common security issue that the cloud customer should consider when allowing users to connect to the cloud with mobile devices?

    A. device registration, authentication, and authorization

    B. office politics

C. candidate screening

D. job rotation

294. Which of the following is not considered a "serverless" cloud configuration, according to the CSA?

   A. application programming interface (API) gateways

   B. data leak protection (DLP) egress monitoring agents

   C. Web servers

   D. notification services

295. A "serverless" cloud architecture places a higher security burden on the _____.

   A. cloud customer

   B. cloud provider

   C. regulator

   D. user

CLOUD CONTROLS MATRIX (CCM)

296. If you wanted to determine whether a certain cloud environment satisfied data backup and recovery requirements, which Domain of the CCM should you refer to?

    A. Governance and Risk Management

    B. Human Resources Security

    C. Mobile Security

    D. Business Continuity Management and Operational Resilience

297. Which Domain of the CCM might be used to determine if a cloud environment is in compliance with ITIL Service Management requirements?

    A. Application and Interface Security

    B. Change Control and Configuration Management

    C. Datacenter Security

    D. Threat and Vulnerability Management

298. Which Domain of the CCM is used to demonstrate the commitment of senior leadership to an information security program?

    A. Audit Assurance and Compliance

    B. Change Control and Configuration Management

    C. Governance and Risk Management

    D. Infrastructure and Virtualization

299. Which Domain of the CCM addresses the roles of employees and contractors in the cloud environment?

    A. Datacenter Security

    B. Human Resources Security

    C. Interoperability and Portability

    D. Supply Chain Management, Transparency, and Accountability

300. Which Domain of the CCM addresses the concept of least privilege?

    A. Application and Interface Security

    B. Audit Assurance and Compliance

    C. Identity and Access Management

    D. Mobile Security

301. Which control listed in the CCM prohibits the use of non-approved applications in the cloud environment?

    A. MOS-03

    B. STA-02

    C. TVM-03

    D. WPA2

302. Which control listed in the CCM recommends using file integrity monitoring when creating an operating system baseline?

    A. GRM-10

    B. HRS-03

    C. IAM-02

    D. IVS-07

303. Which control listed in the CCM discusses policies for encryption key generation?

A. EKM-01

B. EKM-02

C. EKM-03

D. EKM-04

304. Which type of cloud architecture is control HRS-02 applied to? [select all that apply]

   A. Physical

   B. Network

   C. Compute

   D. Storage

   E. Application

   F. Data

305. Which type of cloud architecture is control IAM-11 applied to? [select all that apply]

   A. Physical

   B. Network

   C. Compute

   D. Storage

   E. Application

   F. Data

306. Which type of cloud architecture is control IVS-07 applied to? [select all that apply]

   A. Physical

   B. Network

   C. Compute

D. Storage

E. Application

F. Data

307. According to the CCM, which type of cloud service model requires a mechanism to monitor and quantify the types, volumes, and costs of information security incidents?

    A. IaaS

    B. PaaS

    C. SaaS

    D. All of the above

    E. None of the above

308. According to the CCM, which cloud service model requires that the provider ensure the integrity of all virtual machine images at all times?

    A. IaaS

    B. PaaS

    C. SaaS

    D. All of the above

    E. None of the above

309. According to the CCM, which entity is responsible for ensuring that security vulnerability assessment tools are "virtualization aware"?

    A. the cloud provider

    B. the cloud customer

    C. the regulator

    D. the taxpayer

310. According to the CCM, which entity is responsible for ensuring the

operating system baseline template of a virtualized machine is hardened appropriately?

    A. the cloud provider

    B. the cloud customer

    C. neither the provider nor the customer

    D. both the provider and the customer

311. You are the security officer for a medical college in the United States. Which of the following standards/laws/frameworks from the CCM should most likely apply to your cloud environment? [select all that apply]

    A. PIPEDA

    B. COPPA

    C. FERPA

    D. HIPAA

    E. GDPR

    F. ENISA IAF

312. You are the security officer for a retailer in Germany. Which of the following standards/laws/frameworks from the CCM should most likely apply to your cloud environment? [select all that apply]

    A. NERC CIP

    B. NIST SP 800-53

    C. BSI

    D. GDPR

    E. PCI DSS

313. You are the security officer for a Japanese automotive manufacturer. Which of the following standards/laws/frameworks from the CCM should most likely apply to your cloud environment? [select all that apply].

    A. COBIT

B. ISO 27001

C. FERPA

D. HIPAA

E. GDPR

314. You are the security officer for a charity in Ottawa. Which of the following standards/laws/frameworks from the CCM should most likely apply to your cloud environment? [select all that apply]

A. HIPAA

B. ITAR

C. PIPEDA

D. NZISM

E. NERC CIP

ENISA CLOUD COMPUTING
BENEFITS, RISKS, AND RECOMMENDATIONS FOR INFORMATION SECURITY

315. According to ENISA, is cloud computing a benefit or a risk to security?

    A. benefit

    B. risk

    C. neither

    D. both

316. According to ENISA, which of the following is not one of the top security benefits of cloud computing?

    A. benefits of scale

    B. market differentiation

    C. training opportunities

    D. standardized interfaces

317. According to ENISA, which of the following is not one of the top security risks associated with cloud computing?

    A. insecure or incomplete data deletion

B. wide potential for human error

C. data protection

D. compliance risks

318. According to ENISA, vendor lock-in is rated as a _____ level of risk in the cloud.

   A. high

   B. medium

   C. low

   D. not applicable

319. Which of the following standards is not mentioned by ENISA in the context of secure software assurance?

   A. HIPAA

   B. OWASP

   C. SANS

   D. SAFECode

320. According to ENISA, which is more difficult and less common: attacking the resource isolation mechanisms in a cloud environment (such as the hypervisor), or attacking the operating systems (OSs) in a traditional computing environment?

   A. cloud resource isolation mechanisms

   B. traditional Oss

   C. they are equally difficult and common

   D. neither type of attack ever occurs

321. Which of the following is not an example of an economic denial of service attack against a cloud environment, according to ENISA?

   A. identity theft

B. cache poisoning

C. unexpected resource consumption

D. attacker consuming the customer's metered service

322. Which of the following is not a cloud customer asset that might be affected by the risks associated with licensing, according to ENISA?

    A. company reputation

    B. software

    C. service delivery

    D. certification

323. What is "VM hopping"?

    A. the attacker exceeds the resources of the target VM (such as CPU or RAM)

    B. the attacker makes multiple copies of the target's VM

    C. the attacker deletes the target's VM

    D. the attacker exploits a vulnerability in the hypervisor and can access other VMs

324. Which of the following is not one of the fundamental legal issues associated with all cloud scenarios?

    A. data protection

    B. user training

    C. intellectual property

    D. professional negligence

325. _____ is one way to enhance portability, and avoid vendor lock-in.

    A. use only a single cloud vendor for all cloud computing needs

B. adopt an open standard, such as OVF (the open virtualization standard)

C. use only private clouds

D. use cloud providers only in a single geographic region

326. Which party is typically the data controller, in most cloud service arrangements?

    A. the cloud provider

    B. the cloud customer

    C. the regulator

    D. the data subject

327. Which party is typically the data processor, in most cloud service arrangements?

    A. the cloud provider

    B. the cloud customer

    C. the regulator

    D. the data subject

328. In an IaaS cloud service model, who is responsible for monitoring guest systems?

    A. the auditor

    B. the regulator

    C. the cloud provider

    D. the cloud customer

329. Which of the following is one of the underlying vulnerabilities associated with malicious probes and scans of the cloud environment?

    A. increase in shadow IT

B. social engineering
C. the possibility that internal network probing will occur
D. governmental overreach

DOMAIN 1 ANSWERS

1. Answer: B

   A PaaS model will allow Alice to install, test, and modify software using a variety of OSs, without requiring Alice to install and maintain the OSs.

   If Alice used an IaaS model, she'd have to install and maintain the OSs.

   If Alice used an SaaS model, she wouldn't be able to install, test, or modify her own software.

   As far as I know, there is no Grimbo cloud service model, and this option only exists as a distractor.

2. Answer: B

   A private cloud deployment will offer the most security for the assets you control.

   The other deployment models do not offer the same level of security, and are therefore incorrect.

3. Answer: D

   In an IaaS environment, the customer is responsible for administration of the guest OS.

   The provider would be responsible for the OS in PaaS and SaaS; the regulator and auditor are never responsible for maintaining the OS.

4. Answer: A

   C. While "frangible" is a great word, it is not used to define cloud computing, by either NIST or ISO.

5.   Answer: D

According to the CSA Security Guidance v4 (page 9), orchestration is not a typical element of traditional IT environments, while it is essential to cloud computing.

All the other answers may be part of either cloud or traditional environments.

6.   Answer: A

Traditional IT enterprises are typically designed for a single tenant; most cloud services involve resources shared between multiple tenants.

All the other answers can be included in traditional IT environments (and planning and resiliency definitely should be).

7.   Answer: D

Subsidies are not a typical element of cloud computing.

All the other answers are elements generally associated with cloud computing.

8.   Answer: D

There is no "isolated cloud" deployment model in either the NIST or ISO definitions of cloud computing.

All the other answers are deployment models included in the ISO/NIST definitions.

9.   Answer: C

Page 14 of the CSA Security Guidance v4 explains that most APIs currently use REST.

APIs may or may not the other answers, but those other answers are not listed in the CSA documentation.

10.   Answer: B

Data is stored in the infostructure (CSA Security Guidance, v4, page 19).

All the other answers are parts of the CSA cloud logical model, but don't describe the storage of data.

11.   Answer: C

According to the CSA Security Guidance v4 (page 19), the metastructure describes the fundamental difference between cloud and traditional computing.

All the other answers are parts of the CSA cloud logical model, but don't describe the storage of data.

12.   Answer: C

There is no NCF (I made it up). All the others are models recommended by the CSA (page 22 of the CSA Cloud Security Guidance v4).

13.   Answer: A.

In fact, the cloud provider is responsible for securing the hardware in all cloud deployment models (see page 20 of the CSA Cloud Security Guidance v4).

14.   Answer: A and B

The CSA provides both the CCM and CAIQ to help cloud providers and customers meet regulatory requirements (see page 21 of the CSA Cloud Security Guidance v4).

Diffie-Hellman was created by Diffie and Hellman to help create shared symmetric keys over an untrusted medium, and I made up the Artichoke Incorporation Model.

15.   Answer: B, E, C, G, A, F, D

This is the process described on page 23 of the CSA Security Guidance v4.

16.   Answer: A and B

According to the Cloud Security Alliance (CSA) Security Guidance v4 (page 24), the domains of the Guidance are "divided into two broad categories: governance and operations."

17. Answer: C

All the others are critical focus areas, according to the Cloud Security Alliance (CSA) Security Guidance v4 (page 24).

18. Answer: B

All the others are critical focus areas, according to the Cloud Security Alliance (CSA) Security Guidance v4 (page 25).

19. Answer: C

The CAIQ is offered by the Cloud Security Alliance specifically for that purpose (see page 26 of the Cloud Security Alliance (CSA) Security Guidance v4).

SOX and GDPR are laws, not tools. The STRIDE model is used to assess software security.

20. Answer: B and D

See: the Cloud Security Alliance (CSA) Security Guidance v4 (page 26).

21. Answer: B

B. Cloud-based databases are specifically mentioned as an example of PaaS in the Cloud Security Alliance (CSA) Security Guidance v4 (page 20).

22. Answer: A

See page 14 of the Cloud Security Alliance (CSA) Security Guidance v4.

All the other answers represent risks that could, in fact, pose some potential for the attacker to access/damage your environment, but the management place probably offers the attacker the most opportunity for control/access/damage.

23. Answer: A

NIST SP 800-145 (https://nvlpubs.nist.gov/nistpubs/Legacy/SP/nistspecialpublication800-145.pdf) includes cloud computing definitions and descriptions. These include five essential characteristics (on-demand self-service, broad network access, rapid elasticity, metered service, and resource pooling), three service models (IaaS, PaaS, and SaaS), and four deployment models (private, public, hybrid, and community). See pages 9 and 10 of the Cloud Security Alliance (CSA) Security Guidance v4.

24. Answer: A and D

See page 9 of the Cloud Security Alliance (CSA) Security Guidance v4.

25. Answer: A

See page 21 of the Cloud Security Alliance (CSA) Security Guidance v4. I am sure the other answers are also important, but A is element that is most important, according to the Guidance.

DOMAIN 2 ANSWERS

26. Answer: D

See page 28 of the Cloud Security Alliance (CSA) Security Guidance v4.

27. Answer: B

Every organization is responsible for its own governance. See page 28 of the Cloud Security Alliance (CSA) Security Guidance v4.

Organizations can, and often do, outsource the business functions listed in the other answers.

28. Answer: A

According to the Cloud Security Alliance (CSA) Security Guidance v4 (page 28), cloud providers try to leverage economies of scale for these purposes.

The other answers may, in fact, be things that cloud providers also do, but A is the correct answer according to the Guidance.

29. Answer: B and C

See page 29 of the Cloud Security Alliance (CSA) Security Guidance v4.

30. Answer: B

According to the Cloud Security Alliance (CSA) Security Guidance v4 (page 29), the contract is the only guarantee of service and commitment (aside from legal action).

31. Answer: D

The customer should know what the assessment/audit actually reviewed, not just which standard was used as the basis for the review. See page 30 of the Cloud Security Alliance (CSA) Security Guidance v4.

The inflation rate is a measure of the soundness of a particular currency, and doesn't really have anything to do with audits of cloud providers. The type of hypervisor the provider uses isn't particularly pertinent, as long as the assessment/audit determined whether the appropriate controls were used to secure it (and that those controls are functioning properly). Knowledge of the market isn't critical when reviewing an assessment/audit.

32. Answer: B

The size of the audit effort (or audit provider) is not typically indicative of whether the audit is meaningful and trustworthy.

All the other answers are, in fact, reasons to trust a particular auditor/firm. See page 30 of the Cloud Security Alliance (CSA) Security Guidance v4.

33. Answer: B

The CSA Security, Trust, and Risk program registry is a centralized collection of cloud provider assessments. (See page 30 of the Cloud Security Alliance (CSA) Security Guidance v4.

The CCM and CAIQ are assessment tools used by providers to create content for the STAR Registry. There is no OIP, which I made up.

34. Answer: C

Risk management in the cloud is often described as a shared responsibilities model; the provider is responsible for managing certain risks, while the customer is responsible for others. (See page 30 of the Cloud Security Alliance (CSA) Security Guidance v4.)

The Bell-LaPadula model is an access control model. A covert channel is an attack method for observing target activity. Risk management cannot be totally outsourced.

35. Answer: A and D

The Cloud Security Alliance (CSA) Security Guidance v4 (page 30) specifically notes that good contracts and documentation (from the provider) are essential to enterprise risk management in the cloud.

Neither an equity stake, public interest, nor physical distance of the parties significantly affect risk management.

36. Answer: B

Senior management of each organization will determine the risk tolerance (also referred to as "risk appetite" or "risk threshold") of a particular organization. (See page 31 of the Cloud Security Alliance (CSA) Security Guidance v4.)

37. Answer: C

According to the Cloud Security Alliance (CSA) Security Guidance v4 (page 31), SaaS demonstrates the most critical need for a negotiated contract.

IaaS and PaaS models also require contracts, but those models allow the customer some control of the environment. "BaaS" is not a typical cloud computing model (as defined by NIST/ISO).

38. Answer: A

According to the Cloud Security Alliance (CSA) Security Guidance v4 (page 31), SaaS providers usually are located at each end of the size spectrum.

"Domestic or foreign" literally includes every company on the planet. "Technological or administrative" describes two of the three common types of security controls. "Inflated or conflated" are meaningless words in this context.

39. Answer: A

According to the Cloud Security Alliance (CSA) Security Guidance v4 (page 32), IaaS is the closest approximation of a traditional data center.

QaaS is not a typical service model type, according to the NIST/ISO definition of cloud computing.

40. Answer: D

Because the public cloud serves many different customers, it would be unrealistic for cloud providers to offer unique contracts for every customer (see page 32 of the Cloud Security Alliance (CSA) Security Guidance v4).

Hypervisors and regulators have little to no bearing on whether customers can negotiate cloud contracts. "Inversion" is a meaningless term in this context.

41. Answer: D

Governance for an IT enterprise that extends over multiple environments must cover each environment. See page 33 of the Cloud Security Alliance (CSA) Security Guidance v4).

The physical network, by definition, will not extend into the cloud. The other terms are meaningless in this context.

42. Answer: C

Cloud customers will have less physical access to the IT environment in a public cloud deployment; this reduces risk management options. See page 33 of the Cloud Security Alliance (CSA) Security Guidance v4.

Cloud usage does not affect how much intellectual property an organization deal with. Regulators are not especially hindered or aided in the efforts whether they are reviewing a cloud-based or on-prem environment. Typically, cloud deployments use less electricity, in aggregate, than the sum total of all cloud users (if the cloud users were instead using traditional IT environments).

43. Answer: B

According to page 33 of the Cloud Security Alliance (CSA) Security Guidance v4, technological and process evolution in cloud data centers requires additional customer focus on contract and relationship management.

Cloud providers will evolve data centers without customer input, so A is incorrect. Cloud customers may use employees or contractors regardless of the composition of cloud data centers, so C is incorrect. Cloud users may or may not use personal devices; this is not affected by the technology inside the data center; D is incorrect.

44. Answer: B

See pages 33-34 of the Cloud Security Alliance (CSA) Security Guidance v4. The cloud provider may manage some risks for the cloud customer.

The risk itself cannot be outsourced, nor can the responsibility for managing the risk; this is true for risks due to privacy or any other source. A is incorrect. Providers should not transfer risk to customers, nor accept risk on customers' behalf; C and D are incorrect.

45. Answer: B

Articulation is not a typical method for handling risk; the word is not related to any meaningful activity in our industry, and is only a distractor in this question.

Risk avoidance, transfer, and acceptance are all common industry practices for managing risk. See page 34 of the Cloud Security Alliance (CSA) Security Guidance v4. It is worth noting that there is a typo in the Guidance here: the word "tenant" is used instead of "tenet." This can be confusing, because we typically talk about the cloud as a "multitenant environment," where a tenant is a customer. But the word should be "tenet" in this usage, which means "fundamental premise."

46. Answer: B, A, C, E, D

See page 34 of the Cloud Security Alliance (CSA) Security Guidance v4.

47. Answer: C

Insurance is a form of risk transfer. See page 35 of the Cloud Security Alliance (CSA) Security Guidance v4.

Regulation often increases risk. Governance describes how an organization will manage risk. Postulation has no meaning in this context.

48. Answer: D

The CSA does not suggest that customers renegotiate contract terms after each supplier review, but all the other options are recommended as good practices. (see page 34 of the Cloud Security Alliance (CSA) Security Guidance v4).

49. Answer: D

That is the definition of residual risk: risk that remains after controls are applied.

All the other terms are simply incorrect in this context.

50. Answer: B

Some contracts cannot be negotiated, and are offered without possibility of modification (such as many Terms Of Service for online providers); this should not disqualify those providers as potentially useful. See page 34 of the Cloud Security Alliance (CSA) Security Guidance v4.

All the other options are true/correct, according to the Guidance.

DOMAIN 3 ANSWERS

51. Answer: D

Lawyers will have much more capability to handle legal issues than security practitioners. See page 36 of the CSA Cloud Security Guidance v4.

All the other options may be beneficial, but not as useful as consulting attorneys.

52. Answer: A

The subject is the original owner of privacy data.

All the other options list parties that might be responsible for either protecting the data or the subject's rights, but are not the original owner.

53. Answer: B, G

Privacy laws either cover everyone in a country/region (such as the European Union's General Data Protection Regulation [GDPR]), which are omnibus, or address particular industries/occupations (such as the Health Information Protection and Availability Act [HIPAA] in the US), which are sectoral. See page 38 of the CSA Cloud Security Guidance v4.

The other options are terms that have no meaning in this context.

54. Answer: B

Many privacy laws require that the national laws in countries receiving personal data have similar requirements, and therefore offer individuals an "adequate level of protection." See page 38 of the CSA Cloud Security Guidance v4.

"Reciprocity" suggests both countries honor each other's laws, which would be nice but is not typically the case. I don't know of any laws that require cash payment as part of cross-border transfer. And while encryption and secure storage might be typical controls for personal data, and even included in some privacy laws, "adequate protection" is the more general answer, and therefore more correct in this case.

55. Answer: B

Some privacy laws (such as Russia's and China's) require personal citizen data to be kept within the country which created the law. See page 38 of the CSA Cloud Security Guidance v4.

Privacy laws don't typically specify the format of stored, or whether the data should be stored in a traditional or cloud environment.

56. Answer: D

The US does not have an omnibus personal privacy law; instead, personal privacy in the US is addressed by a patchwork of sectoral federal and state laws.

Australia, the EU, and Argentina all have strict personal privacy laws (and some have more than one).

57. Answer: C

Japan has sectoral laws instead of an omnibus federal personal privacy law. See page 40 of the CSA Cloud Security Guidance v4.

China, Canada, and Chile all have omnibus federal personal privacy laws.

58. Answer: B

The GDPR is applicable globally. How this may affect questions of national sovereignty has yet to be determined. See pages 41-42 of the CSA Cloud Security Guidance v4.

All the other options are true statements about the GDPR.

59. Answer: A

See page 42 of the CSA Cloud Security Guidance v4.

60. Answer: B

The cap for penalties is 20 million euros. See page 42 of the CSA Cloud Security Guidance v4.

61. Answer: D

International law creates a legal obligation, not a contractual obligation. All the other options are sources of contractual obligations. See page 45 of the CSA Cloud Security Guidance v4.

62. Answer: D

Under most privacy laws, the organization that originally collected or created the sensitive data set is legally responsible for the disposition of that data, to include any loss of that data caused by a third party.

The cloud provider might also have some liability, depending on the nature of the loss, but the organization that shared the data with the provider retains most of the liability. Neither the data subject nor the regulator(s) have any liability for unauthorized disclosure.

63. Answer: C

According to the CSA Cloud Security Guidance v4 (page 41), the subject must provide specific, informed, and unambiguous consent in order for data processing to be legal.

The other options don't really suit this particular context, and aren't elements of the subject's interaction with the controller.

64. Answer: B

Performing due diligence can reduce liability by averting accusations of negligence.

Due diligence might also lead to enhanced profitability, increased public esteem, or perhaps counter certain attacks, but this is not a direct effect, and B is the better answer.

65. Answer: C

The purpose of the scope (or "scoping statement") is to describe the features, services, and systems covered in the audit/assessment. See page 48 of the CSA Cloud Security Guidance v4.

The other options may be parts of the audit/assessment report, but do not typically include a description of the features/services which were covered.

66. Answer: D

By and large, hackers will not negotiate contracts with their victims; even in the cases where hackers will offer to negotiate (such as in ransomware attacks), hackers generally should not be trusted to fulfill their contracts in good faith. All the other options are risks that can be reduced by negotiated good contracts. See page 48 of the CSA Cloud Security Guidance v4.

67. Answer: B

Public cloud providers are particularly prone to offering non-negotiable contract terms. See page 48 of the CSA Cloud Security Guidance v4.

Contracts should not be excessive, illegal, or ludicrous.

68. Answer: B

Audits and attestations are used to demonstrate compliance with standards. See page 48 of the CSA Cloud Security Guidance v4.

Audits/attestations typically do not portray a target's agreement, contract, or membership with a standard or standards body.

69. Answer: C

This is the definition of "discovery." See page 48 of the CSA Cloud Security Guidance v4.

"Invasion" and "surveillance" are not common legal terms. "Seizure" is typically only performed by law enforcement entities, government bodies, or courts, not by opposing counsel during litigation.

70. Answer: A

This is the doctrine of "adverse inference," and is a good reason to ensure that data discovery is performed in a thorough and careful manner. See pages 48-49 of the CSA Cloud Security Guidance v4.

71. Answer: B

This is a nuanced question, because "overpreserve" is the correct answer (see page 50 of the CSA Cloud Security Guidance v4), the process might involve copying information, so the reader might tend toward answer C. However, B is the more correct and applicable response.

During discovery, preservation, and disclosure, it is not typical for a participant to destroy or interpret data.

72. Answer: D

The cloud customer does not typically have access to hardware in the cloud data center, for a variety of reasons. See page 51 of the CSA Cloud Security Guidance v4.

Laws do not typically stipulate the form of data preservation.

73. Answer: B

Discovery and disclosure rarely require providing opposing counsel direct access to the IT environment. See page 52 of the CSA Cloud Security Guidance v4.

It is likely that litigants would be aware of and have some familiarity with the cloud IT environment of each party, and "working knowledge" is not pertinent in this context.

74. Answer: A

A notification requirement is a useful aspect of a contract, when, where, and if it is allowed in the relevant jurisdictions. See page 53 of the CSA Cloud Security Guidance v4.

Cloud providers have no legal standing to deny or resist legal evidentiary requests. Whether or not the provider retains an attorney is irrelevant.

75.   Answer: B

The CSA recommends information from the Sedona Conference for those interested in evidentiary matters related to electronic data. See page 53 of the CSA Cloud Security Guidance v4.

OWASP is an excellent resource for web security knowledge, but is not particularly pertinent to the topic of electronic evidence. Your local library may or may not have information about evidentiary matters. It is a terrible idea to wait until litigation occurs to begin preparing for legal action.

DOMAIN 4 ANSWERS

76. Answer: C

See page 54 of the CSA Cloud Security Guidance v4. Laws (and lawmakers) typically lag several years behind technological innovation and evolution.

77. Answer: B and E

Because cloud computing resources are typically virtualized and distributed, traditional audit approaches may not be applicable. See page 54 of the CSA Cloud Security Guidance v4.

The self-service, resilient, and metered service aspects of cloud computing do not generally affect audit methodologies. Cloud computing services are not typically "physical" in the manner of traditional IT environments; this is the opposite of the correct answer.

78. Answer: B

Typically, organizations might choose internal or external audits, or both.

The speed or hour that audits take place are not typically used to distinguish types of audits. Audits should not be illegal.

79. Answer: B

The cloud customer is ultimately (legally) responsible for ensuring compliance with a given standard/regulation/law. See page 55 of the CSA Cloud Security Guidance v4.

The provider may perform some compliance actions on behalf of the customer, but the customer retains legal liability/responsibility. Regulators enforce and monitor compliance, but are not ultimately responsible for a customer's compliance. The data subject is not responsible for compliance.

80. Answer: D

The cloud customer is generally not allowed to perform their own audit of a cloud provider's environment, and probably should not trust the provider's self-reporting (as it is inherently biased), so third-party attestation is perhaps the sole method of ensuring compliance in the cloud. See page 56 of the CSA Cloud Security Guidance v4.

Customers also cannot rely on regulators to perform this function on their behalf, nor the efforts of news media.

81. Answer: A

This is the definition of compliance inheritance, also known as a pass-through audit. See page 56 of the CSA Cloud Security Guidance v4.

Regulatory capture is the term used to describe conflicts of interest in relationships between regulators and the industry they are meant to regulate. The other two terms are meaningless in this context.

82. Answer: B

The cloud customer remains responsible for regulatory compliance of their own environment/app when using inherited compliance/pass-through audits in the cloud. See page 56 of the CSA Cloud Security Guidance v4.

83. Answer: B

The CISSP is a certification for personnel, not cloud providers. All the others are often used as third-party attestations for pass-through compliance in the cloud. See page 56 of the CSA Cloud Security Guidance v4.

84. Answer: C

See page 57 of the CSA Cloud Security Guidance v4.

Customers will not typically be allowed to audit cloud data centers. Audits are not illegal in any jurisdiction I am aware of. Cloud providers do not typically try to deceive customers.

85. Answer: A

Auditors should, in general, not make vendor recommendations, as that creates the appearance of conflict of interest.

All the other responses are elements included in most audit reports. See page 57 of the CSA Cloud Security Guidance v4.

86. Answer: D

Payment is typically an accounting function, not usually included in audit management.

All the other responses are functions of audit management. See page 57 of the CSA Cloud Security Guidance v4.

87. Answer: D

Audit reports may contain sensitive information about the target's IT environment and/or security measures. See page 58 of the CSA Cloud Security Guidance v4.

Prospective customers should not have to pay to see audit results, and generally are not entering the same market as the provider, so the other answers are incorrect.

88. Answer: B

Some types of audits/assessments (such as vulnerability scans or penetration tests) may be mistaken for an attack if not coordinated with the provider in advance. See page 58 of the CSA Cloud Security Guidance v4.

"Competitive influence" suggests another cloud provider reviewing the target; this would be a form of attack, and B is the better, more general answer. The provider should be able to determine if a particular activity is internal or part of normal customer operations without prior coordination.

89. Answer: C

See page 58 of the CSA Cloud Security Guidance v4.

90. Answer: C

See page 59 of the CSA Cloud Security Guidance v4.

Not all audits are entertaining, expensive, or remote (some are done on-site, most are dull, and a few are affordable).

91. Answer: C

It is the customer's duty to ensure the provider's third-party reports meet the customer's needs. See page 59 of the CSA Cloud Security Guidance v4.

92. Answer: D

The CCM is useful for this purpose. See page 59 of the CSA Cloud Security Guidance v4.

The NIST SP 800-145 just defines cloud computing, the SSAE 18 is an audit standard (used by auditors), and the GDPR is a privacy law.

93. Answer: C

Compliance gaps can expose customers to additional, unpredicted, risks. See page 59 of the CSA Cloud Security Guidance v4.

Continual compliance does not aid in reducing any of the elements mentioned in the other responses.

94. Answer: B

Logs are considered compliance artifacts. See pages 58 and 59 of the CSA Cloud Security Guidance v4.

Contracts, regulations, and laws are not considered compliance artifacts.

95. Answer: B

Cloud providers could not reasonably grant physical access to hundreds (or possibly thousands) of different customers. See page 58 of the CSA Cloud Security Guidance v4.

96. Answer: C

Security controls are often required for compliance, and the security practitioner is tasked with ensuring those controls are functioning properly and achieving the intended goal. See page 55 of the CSA Cloud Security Guidance v4.

The security practitioner may (and should) perform the other activities listed, but those activities are not as directly essential for compliance.

97. Answer: A

The jurisdiction of both the cloud provider and customer will have significant impact on which standards/laws/regulations all parties are required to comply with. See page 54 of the CSA Cloud Security Guidance v4.

The other responses do not typically affect compliance requirements.

98. Answer: B

This is the definition and purpose of GRC. The others are industry terms, but not relevant to this topic. See page 55 of the CSA Cloud Security Guidance v4.

99. Answer: C

X509 is not a mandate, and an organization does not have to commission audits for it, unlike the other responses. Organizations follow the X509 standard because universal acceptance is mutually beneficial, not because a regulator will verify compliance.

100. Answer: A

Audit and assurance are part of organizational governance efforts. See page 57 of the CSA Cloud Security Guidance v4.

DOMAIN 5 ANSWERS

101. Answer: B

All the other responses are typical governance domains affected by cloud computing. See page 62 of the CSA Cloud Security Guidance v4.

102. Answer: C

All the other responses are typical governance domains affected by cloud computing. See page 62 of the CSA Cloud Security Guidance v4.

103. Answer: D

All the other responses are typical governance domains affected by cloud computing. See page 62 of the CSA Cloud Security Guidance v4.

104. Answer: C, F, D, A, E, B

See page 63 of the CSA Cloud Security Guidance v4.

105. Answer: B

"Write" would be considered an aspect of "process." See page 65 of the CSA Cloud Security Guidance v4.

106. Answer: C

Typically, the data owner will be the entity creating/collecting the original dataset, and will therefore be in charge of assigning security controls. See page 63 of the CSA Cloud Security Guidance v4.

The subject, regulators, and processor are typically not responsible for the Create phase.

107. Answer: C

The Store phase occurs as soon as data is entered in electronic format; for the majority of data created today, this will be the moment the data is collected or created, which is the Create phase. The other phases may occur later, or may not occur at all. See page 63 of the CSA Cloud Security Guidance v4.

108. Answer: D

Cryptoshredding is the practice of using encryption to securely sanitize a data space; this would be at the end of the Lifecycle, in the Destroy phase. See page 63 of the CSA Cloud Security Guidance v4.

109. Answer: C

In the Archive phase, data is removed from the production environment but still kept in storage. This is an excellent description of backups. See page 63 of the CSA Cloud Security Guidance v4.

110. Answer: D, E

The customer's interests may be protected through favorable contract terms or through the use of the customer's own security controls. See page 66 of the CSA Cloud Security Guidance v4.

The customer will not typically be allowed to implement physical security controls in the cloud environment. Notional or voluntary controls would not be effective. "Reprisal controls" are not a common industry term, and is only used here as a distractor. Controls do not need to be expensive to be effective.

111. Answer: A

There is a significant likelihood that an organization that previously only maintained data in a traditional environment does not already have proper governance/policy for the involvement of third parties. Because cloud computing requires third-party management of data, the organizational will have to modify existing governance/policy to reflect the change. See page 66 of the CSA Cloud Security Guidance v4.

Cloud migration does not typically require significant initial investment, so securing additional funding is not a usually pre-migration activity. Most organizations do not require public permission for operational business decisions. ICANN does not offer "cloud licenses."

112. Answer: B

This is the intended purpose of the Data Security Lifecycle. See page 66 of the CSA Cloud Security Guidance v4.

The CCM is used to verify security compliance across multiple standards/regulations. The CAIQ is used to report/assess a given environment's controls satisfy requirements. NIST SP 800-37 is the Risk Management Framework (RMF).

113. Answer: B

According to the CSA Cloud Security Guidance v4 (page 65), a device is not considered an actor.

114. Answer: C

Data transmitted from one user to another is considered an aspect of the Share phase. See page 63 of the CSA Cloud Security Guidance v4.

115. Answer: B

The Data Security Lifecycle is not strictly applicable to every process in every organization; it is a tool that may be useful for modeling data handling and security controls. See page 63 of the CSA Cloud Security Guidance v4.

116. Answer: C

The contract is the means by which an organization can impose governance requirements on external parties, such as the cloud customer/provider relationship. See page 62 of the CSA Cloud Security Guidance v4.

117. Answer: A

The cloud customer retains ownership of data entrusted to it, even if the data is sent to/processed/stored in the cloud by a cloud provider. See page 62 of the CSA Cloud Security Guidance v4.

118. Answer: D

Attorneys will be best situated to understand legal implications of the operating in multiple jurisdictions. See page 62 of the CSA Cloud Security Guidance v4.

119. Answer: B and C

See page 60 of the CSA Cloud Security Guidance v4.

120. Answer: B

This is the definition included on page 60 of the CSA Cloud Security Guidance v4.

DOMAIN 6 ANSWERS

121. Answer: D

All the other responses may exist in the traditional IT environment, but the management plane is unique to cloud computing. See page 67 of the CSA Cloud Security Guidance v4.

122. Answer: D

This is particularly true for IaaS environments, which very much replicate the function and purpose of the traditional data center. See page 67 of the CSA Cloud Security Guidance v4.

Both access to personnel records and physical access to the building may result in damage to the organization, but are somewhat limited, and not nearly the level of threat posed by illicit access to the management plane. Monitoring inbound and outbound traffic poses a significant risk, but not nearly on the scale of what an attacker could by controlling the management plane.

123. Answer: B

The customer creates the credentials used to access the management plane, and is responsible for securing and managing them. See page 68 of the CSA Cloud Security Guidance v4.

124. Answer: D

Trying to change or create laws is not a typical security activity. The other responses are the main aspects of cloud BCDR. See page 68 of the CSA Cloud Security Guidance v4.

125. Answer: B

It is difficult to build multiple traditional data centers in different geographic areas, as physical property is very expensive. In the cloud, however, spreading virtual resources across different physical locations is efficient and cost-effective. See page 68 of the CSA Cloud Security Guidance v4.

126. Answer: A

In an IaaS cloud, the customer has much more authority and responsibility to configure the cloud environment. See page 69 of the CSA Cloud Security Guidance v4.

"Public" is a deployment model, not a service model.

127. Answer: A, B, C

The most expensive service is not always optimum for your business goals. All the other responses are advised by the CSA. See page 69 of the CSA Cloud Security Guidance v4.

128. Answer: B

In an SaaS model, the customer typically has minimal interaction with the environment, often typified by an "admin" or "settings" tab on the interface. See page 69 of the CSA Cloud Security Guidance v4.

The other responses are not at all typical for SaaS customers; A and D almost never are granted to customers, and C is usually restricted to PaaS and IaaS customers.

129. Answer: C, D

IaaS architecture can be used to enhance logical separation and process/system isolation. See page 69 of the CSA Cloud Security Guidance v4.

The management plane does not aid with refraction or navigation, which are terms with no meaning in this context. The management plane does not aid in compensation (payment); payment is usually based on performance.

130. Answer: A, F

See page 69 of the CSA Cloud Security Guidance v4. The management plane will be used by the cloud provider to set up and optimize the cloud infrastructure, and also by the cloud customer, to apportion the IT resources they've paid to access.

The management plane is not typically accessed by auditors, government agents, or regulators, and end users do not typically get physical access to the cloud data center.

131. Answer: B,C

See page 69 of the CSA Cloud Security Guidance v4.

132. Answer: A

See page 70 of the CSA Cloud Security Guidance v4.

133. Answer: C

While the customization may include the organization's color scheme and logo, it's the domain name that actually directs that organization's users to a customized interface for the web console. See page 70 of the CSA Cloud Security Guidance v4.

Cloud management plane web consoles should not be browser-dependent.

134. Answer: B

According to page 70 of the CSA Cloud Security Guidance v4, "REST is easy to implement over the Internet." SOAP (a protocol based on XML) can also be used to create APIs, but is not as modern as REST.

135. Answer: D

Both REST and HTTP were created by the same person, Roy Fielding. See page 70 of the CSA Cloud Security Guidance v4.

Fiber and wifi are communications media; most protocols can run over most media. "All obstacles" is a distractor here.

136. Answer: B, D

Both of these use cryptography to enhance authentication. See page 70 of the CSA Cloud Security Guidance v4.

Ticket-granting tickets are a characteristic of Kerberos. "Quad processors" and "large fonts" are just distractors in this context.

137. Answer: B

Isolation is not an element of IAM. See page 70 of the CSA Cloud Security Guidance v4.

138. Answer: D

Typically, recovery of lost accounts (or credentials) should involve a complicated process that includes identity challenges and additional authorization confirmation. See page 71 of the CSA Cloud Security Guidance v4.

139. Answer: B

See page 71 of the CSA Cloud Security Guidance v4.

Alphanumeric passphrases with special characters that are 16-characters long are good, but multiple factors for authentication is a better means to achieve security. XML is a distractor in this context.

140. Answer: D

See page 71 of the CSA Cloud Security Guidance v4. MFA addresses many kinds of attacks.

Firewalls typically protect against hostile inbound logical attacks. Cameras only protect against physical attacks. Egress monitoring typically protects against data exfiltration.

141. Answer: A

A pooled environment is typically complex, and any particular virtual instance/workload/machine may be prone to loss or failure. See page 73 of the CSA Cloud Security Guidance v4.

This should not have any effect (or be affected by) the location of the customers, the communications/networking media used, or the certification of the systems.

142. Answer: D

BCDR is one of the purposes for using SDI. See page 73 of the CSA Cloud Security Guidance v4.

APIs and AI don't necessarily aid in the use/creation of templates. "Intrinsic motivation" is a nonsense term in this context.

143. Answer: A

Replicating cloud assets across multiple geographic regions is typically more expensive that hosting a cloud environment in a single location. See page 74 of the CSA Cloud Security Guidance v4.

Laws may or may not restrict cross-border data transfer, but BCDR replication can be done within a single country/jurisdiction. The location of cloud assets should be irrelevant to users. The color scheme of the web console is of very little importance (usually) when planning BCDR responses.

144. Answer: D

This methodology was pioneered and popularized by Netflix, which created a series of automated agents called the SIMian Army, including a Chaos Monkey and a Chaos Gorilla (https://netflixtechblog.com/the-netflix-simian-army-16e57fbab116?gi=e48688837c22). Netflix has since made these tools available to the public, for free (https://github.com/Netflix/SimianArmy). See page 74 of the CSA Cloud Security Guidance v4.

All of the other responses are terms I just made up, and used as distractors.

145. Answer: B

Because loss of availability is always a possibility, the cloud customer should design the architecture for graceful failure-- that is, no additional impact should be realized after the outage occurs. See page 76 of the CSA Cloud Security Guidance v4.

If BCDR response is planned appropriately, loss of availability should not lead to bankruptcy, cataclysm, or legal action.

DOMAIN 7 ANSWERS

146. Answer: D

There is no "review" network in typical cloud data centers. See page 78 of the CSA Cloud Security Guidance v4.

147. Answer: B, E

VLAN and SDN are the two general categories of network virtualization used in modern cloud computing. See pages 78-79 of the CSA Cloud Security Guidance v4.

SaaS is a service model, not a type of network virtualization. A hypervisor is used to create virtual instances. "Perforated" is meaningless in this context. "TPS" is a fake term made up as a distractor.

148. Answer: A

SDNs allow network abstraction away from the hardware and data stored therein. See page 79 of the CSA Cloud Security Guidance v4.

The network is still tethered to the data center and Internet, and the customer can still access the data through the SDN.

149. Answer: D, E

See page 79 of the CSA Cloud Security Guidance v4.

SDNs do not typically cost more than other cloud options (and may actually cost less), nor do they entail more risk or regulation. "Abridgement" has no meaning in this context and is only a distractor.

150. Answer: B

Customers can use SDNs to grow an existing (on-premise) network into the cloud by assigning IP addresses that use the existing range. See page 79 of the CSA Cloud Security Guidance v4.

SDNs do not typically use proprietary data formats or specific hardware, nor do they limit interaction with other networks (these would actually be detrimental to cloud usage, instead of aiding the effort).

151. Answer: C

SDNs utilize encapsulation so that various assets can communicate across a networked environment without any other changes or customization. See page 79 of the CSA Cloud Security Guidance v4.

AC is a means to deliver electricity, not information. DLP is used to monitor data (not deliver it). "Rarified prohibition" is a nonsense term used as a distractor here.

152. Answer: D

Customers cannot get physical access to the network in most cloud computing arrangements, which severely limits the customer's use of security controls typical in the traditional environment. See page 79 of the CSA Cloud Security Guidance v4.

All the other responses describe situations that exist in both the cloud and traditional environments, so don't pose any novel difficulties.

153. Answer: C

Virtual appliances used for security purposes may cause traffic bottlenecks, because they cannot fail open in the same manner a hardware security device would. See page 80 of the CSA Cloud Security Guidance v4.

The use of virtual appliances for security in the cloud environment should be transparent to end users, not affect availability of other systems, and come with a fixed price.

154. Answer: D

If the vendors of the product do not allow the customer to replicate the appliance as needed under the licensing terms, the organization using that appliance may have limited elasticity. See page 80 of the CSA Cloud Security Guidance v4.

Virtual appliances used for security purposes should typically handle fluctuating traffic and user base, and have the technical capacity for creating new instances.

155. Answer: C

In the cloud environment, IP addresses are subject to change far more frequently than in a traditional enterprise, so the use of unique IDs is preferable. See page 80 of the CSA Cloud Security Guidance v4.

156. Answer: B

Granular is the best option of these responses; SDN firewalls allow extreme specificity of traffic to or from particular assets in the environment, regardless of the physical location of the asset on the network. See page 80 of the CSA Cloud Security Guidance v4.

The use of SDN firewalls may or may not be simple, expensive, or immediate.

157. Answer: B

SDN firewalls are usually default-deny. See page 80 of the CSA Cloud Security Guidance v4.

SDN firewalls are not typically free of charge. They are, however, usually quite effective, and allow for granular control (as opposed to broad effect).

158. Answer: B

Microsegmentation allows for application isolation in a cost-effective manner. See page 82 of the CSA Cloud Security Guidance v4.

There should be many virtual networks inside a data center and an organization. Putting each user on a distinct network has no real advantage.

159. Answer: D

Colloquially referred to as "reducing the blast radius" in the CSA Cloud Security Guidance v4, this is discussed on page 84.

Microsegmentation doesn't add an extra layer of access control on a file (that actually describes digital rights management)), or block DDOS attacks. It may help in limiting impact from a rogue or careless administrator, but D is the better answer.

160. Answer: D

Microsegmentation may require additional administrative and managerial efforts, which are operational expenses. See page 82 of the CSA Cloud Security Guidance v4.

Additional virtual network segments do not incur more investment, so is not a capital expenditure. Likewise, microsegmentation does not add more risk or regulation.

161. Answer: B

There is no "SDP motivator" defined by the SDP Working Group. All the other responses are elements of the SDP model. See page 82 of the CSA Cloud Security Guidance v4.

162. Answer: B

DRM is a file-based access control mechanism, and would not aid in network separation. The other options are all recommended by CSA. See page 83 of the CSA Cloud Security Guidance v4.

163. Answer: B

The cost of registering domain names is not significantly increased by hybrid cloud deployments. All the other options are challenges involved with hybrid clouds. See page 83 of the CSA Cloud Security Guidance v4.

164. Answer: A

Each second-level network can only connect to the data center through the dedicated bastion/transit network/VPN, and therefore isolated from each other. See page 84 of the CSA Cloud Security Guidance v4.

Users are still able to reach the cloud (otherwise the cloud would be kind of pointless). Bastion/transit virtual networks don't really aid in preventing DOS/DDOS attacks, nor in authentication.

165.   Answer: C, E

Workloads are units of processing (see page 84 of the CSA Cloud Security Guidance v4). This can include any abstracted assets, including containers and virtual machines.

Workloads are not data, files, companies, people, or people.

166.   Answer: A, B

As abstracted processing assets, workloads will always consume memory and run on processors. See page 84 of the CSA Cloud Security Guidance v4.

Workloads may or may not cross borders, depending on how the cloud architecture is deployed in the cloud environment. Workloads aren't typically the cause of user error (but may be impacted by it).

167.   Answer: B

Containers use the kernel of an existing OS, and therefore don't need to boot another OS to launch. See page 85 of the CSA Cloud Security Guidance v4.

Containers may or may not use SSDs; they can use other media as well. "Neutrino memory" is only a distractor here, and has no actual meaning. The popularity of containers does not make them fast; the opposite is probably true (the speed of containers makes them popular).

168.   Answer: C

This is the job of the cloud provider. See page 86 of the CSA Cloud Security Guidance v4.

169.   Answer: A

In an environment using immutable workloads, patches are not applied to individual virtual machines; instead, the core ("golden") image is updated, and new versions of that image are instantiated in place of the old instances, which are destroyed. See page 86 of the CSA Cloud Security Guidance v4.

Immutability may or may not be "legal" (and is rarely a matter of law), and does not make images/instances unsusceptible to malware infection. Unfortunately, nothing in the world can prevent user error.

170. Answer: A

All instances/workloads will be formed during the creation (and updating) of the golden image; therefore, the golden image must be consistently and regularly updated with all current patches and fixes in order to ensure the environment is properly protected. See page 87 of the CSA Cloud Security Guidance v4.

What you pay your engineers or where you are located should not necessarily have direct impact on immutable environments. Auditors do not approve architectures; auditors ensure compliance with a standard.

DOMAIN 8 ANSWERS

171. Answer: C

In a multitenant cloud environment, if one process could observe another process, or capture data from another process, one cloud customer might gain unauthorized access to other customers. See page 93 of the CSA Cloud Security Guidance v4.

Process isolation might, in fact, aid a cloud provider or customer with compliance for a given standard/regulation, but this is an outcome, not a reason. Process isolation, like all good security practices, will have a negative impact on cost and efficiency.

172. Answer: B

Typically, cloud customers do not have access to personnel files for cloud provider employees. See pages 93-94 of the CSA Cloud Security Guidance v4.

All the other answers are examples of security controls commonly available to cloud customers.

173. Answer: C

We cannot yet virtualize users in most environments. See pages 92, 94, and 97 of the CSA Cloud Security Guidance v4.

174. Answer: C

See page 94 of the CSA Cloud Security Guidance v4. Clouds are often multitenant environments, so process/data isolation is crucial.

There is no appreciable difference between VLANs and SDNs in terms of cost, regulatory restriction, and speed.

175. Answer: A

This is a difficult question. While C may be true (some regulators might require sensitive processes to run in a traditional environment, or may disallow cloud operations), this is the cause of network monitoring devices having less effectiveness in the cloud. A is correct and true. See page 96 of the CSA Cloud Security Guidance v4.

Auditors can review any artifact that is presented to them, including virtualized instances. As far as I know, no jurisdiction has outlawed the use of network monitoring tools in cloud environments; again, this would not be a reason that those tools were less effective.

176. Answer: B

Public cloud providers offer native, cloud-based firewall solutions to accomplish the monitoring tasks that physical firewalls are intended for; these may be a viable option for the cloud customer. See page 96 of the CSA Cloud Security Guidance v4.

While strong contract language is useful in any cloud arrangement, it does not accomplish the same goals that firewalls are meant to accomplish. Likewise, DRM and user training are good practices, and may be used in conjunction with firewalls for defense in depth, they do not offer network monitoring.

177. Answer: B

In a multitenant environment, ensuring that customers cannot see each other's traffic is absolutely essential. See page 96 of the CSA Cloud Security Guidance v4.

While maximum bandwidth and optimizing APIs are useful to customers, those typically are performance goals, not security goals. The provider protecting its own intellectual property is more about profitability for the provider, and not a paramount security function.

178. Answer: C

This is the definition of an overlay network. See page 97 of the CSA Cloud Security Guidance v4.

VLANs are used to segment networks. Wifi is a term used to describe the IEEE standard 802.11 for wireless networking (and is actually a trademark of the Wi-Fi Alliance). "Maximal networking" is only a distractor, and has no meaning in this context.

179. Answer: C, F

Both SAN and NAS are often used in traditional enterprises. See page 97 of the CSA Cloud Security Guidance v4.

HTTP is used for Web traffic. VLANs are used to segment networks. "Hippo" is purely invented, and has no meaning in this context. Apache is a Web server technology.

180. Answer: B

This is one of the many purposes of encryption. See page 97 of the CSA Cloud Security Guidance v4.

Watermarking does not prevent data from being revealed; instead, it is used to assert ownership rights when data is revealed. "Superimposition" is only a distractor, and has no meaning in this context. Steganography is embedding a message of one medium in another, often to convey the message in plain sight.

181. Answer: A

This is a definition of a container. See page 97 of the CSA Cloud Security Guidance v4.

Web servers host and portray web content. Kerberos is a single sign-on solution. OAuth is an identity federation standard.

182. Answer: D

Containers provide isolated areas for individual users, but share the same underlying kernel. See page 97 of the CSA Cloud Security Guidance v4.

"Vernacular" has no meaning in this context; "molecular bond" is a chemistry term-- both are used here only as distractors. Containers do not typically include an entire OS.

183.   Answer: C

Data encrypted at the virtualization layer may still be exposed to the cloud provider, because the provider has access to the underlying infrastructure, and possibly the encryption mechanism. See page 97 of the CSA Cloud Security Guidance v4.

We generally aren't using encryption to protect data from users; users need access to the data in order to be productive. Data encrypted at the virtualization layer should be protected from external attack. We also don't typically use encryption to protect data from regulators, because they need to see some data.

184.   Answer: B

A GUI is not one of the typical crucial components of a software container system; all the other answers are. See page 98 of the CSA Cloud Security Guidance v4.

185.   Answer: D

Typically, code is not encrypted as it runs. All the other answers are security measures that should be used to protect containerized environments. See page 98 of the CSA Cloud Security Guidance v4.

186.   Answer: A

Role-based access controls and strong authentication are considered the bare minimum security features that should be included in container solutions. See page 98 of the CSA Cloud Security Guidance v4.

All the other answers are examples of good security practices, but which might not be included with (or enforced by) containers.

187.   Answer: C

In order to totally comprehend containers, you must have a thorough knowledge of operating system mechanisms. See page 99 of the CSA Cloud Security Guidance v4.

The other answers are topics which are worth knowing, but which do not necessarily aid in deep knowledge of container technology.

188. Answer: B

Divestiture is a management function, where a business unit is sold or otherwise released from the organization. All the other answers are elements of an operating system. See page 99 of the CSA Cloud Security Guidance v4.

189. Answer: C

See page 99 of the CSA Cloud Security Guidance v4.

190. Answer: C

See page 99 of the CSA Cloud Security Guidance v4.

191. Answer: A

See page 100 of the CSA Cloud Security Guidance v4.

192. Answer: A

See page 100 of the CSA Cloud Security Guidance v4.

193. Answer: D

This is the definition of the purpose of auditing.

194. Answer: B

Cloud customers are expected to keep their own credentials secure. All the other answers are typical security responsibilities for the cloud provider. See page 99 of the CSA Cloud Security Guidance v4.

195. Answer: A

This is essential to protecting customer data from malicious/rogue cloud administrators; if the provider is providing encryption services to the customer, these services must be distinct from the data-management function. See page 100 of the CSA Cloud Security Guidance v4.

The cloud provider is not responsible for training cloud customer personnel; B is incorrect. DRM would not prevent cloud provider administrators from accessing customer data stored in the cloud; C is incorrect. D is a responsibility of the cloud customer (and would not necessarily protect the data from cloud provider employees).

DOMAIN 9 ANSWERS

196. Answer: D

The CSA Guidance uses NIST SP 800-61 to describe the incident response process. See page 101 of the CSA Cloud Security Guidance v4.

Answers A and B are both industry-accepted standards used for incident response process modeling, but are not used by CSA for this purpose in the Guidance. Answer C is completely made up, and used here only as a distractor.

197. Answer: B

The other answers are phases described in the Guidance. See page 102 of the CSA Cloud Security Guidance v4.

198. Answer: D

The other answers are from the second and third phases of the incident response lifecycle. See page 102 of the CSA Cloud Security Guidance v4.

199. Answer: D

The post-mortem phase is used to optimize incident handling and response. See page 103 of the CSA Cloud Security Guidance v4.

200. Answer: D

All of the phases of the incident response process are affected by cloud operations. See page 103 of the CSA Cloud Security Guidance v4.

201. Answer: B

While joint training sessions may be a good idea, it is impractical and implausible to expect. All the other answers are recommendations made by the CSA. See page 103 of the CSA Cloud Security Guidance v4.

202. Answer: B

Incident response log data may be limited to log data already provided prior to the incident, and additional requests might not be honored; the customer needs to understand the scope and availability of logs, as defined by the contract. See page 103 of the CSA Cloud Security Guidance v4.

Physical security and devices are typically opaque to the customer; these are the responsibility of the provider; A and D are incorrect. All user access to the cloud is remote access; C is incorrect.

203. Answer: B

Nothing is 100% (risk or security or availability or anything else); avoid any provider that offers a metric of 100% (or 0%). All the other answers are methods a cloud customer should use to optimize the effectiveness of incident response actions. See page 104 of the CSA Cloud Security Guidance v4.

204. Answer: B and C

Threat modeling and tabletop exercises can aid the organization in determining if the cloud architecture is optimized for incident containment activities. See page 104 of the CSA Cloud Security Guidance v4.

User training and protecting credentials are useful in protecting the cloud environment, but do not aid in reviewing the architecture for incident response actions. Provider billing has nothing to do with incident response.

205. Answer: B

Close observation of the cloud management console might allow the customer to determine if unauthorized/unscheduled configuration changes have occurred. See page 104 of the CSA Cloud Security Guidance v4

Customers aren't typically able to install hardware appliances in the cloud environment; A is incorrect. DRM and strong contract language are both useful for protecting the customer, but not for monitoring configuration changes; C and D are incorrect.

206. Answer: A

External threat intelligence is always useful, whether the customer runs a traditional IT environment or cloud environment. See page 105 of the CSA Cloud Security Guidance v4.

The other answers are all incorrect, and somewhat silly, if not downright counterproductive and/or illegal.

207. Answer: C

Nobody will be more prepared to answer legal questions than lawyers. See page 105 of the CSA Cloud Security Guidance v4.

208. Answer: D

Automation reduces the potential for human and leverages the power of IT solutions. See page 105 of the CSA Cloud Security Guidance v4.

209. Answer: C

Alert review is one task that requires human intervention; no automation tool can yet approximate human capabilities in this regard. See page 105 of the CSA Cloud Security Guidance v4.

All the other answers are tasks that can be automated.

210. Answer: A and D

Both of these are potential ways to gauge the impact of a given incident. See page 105 of the CSA Cloud Security Guidance v4.

B and C are both characteristics of cloud computing, but not particularly useful in determining the extent of incident impact. E is not intrinsically related to cloud computing, nor is it useful to ascertain the impact of an incident.

211. Answer: B

An attacker with administrative access to the management console can subvert any other incident response actions the customer might try; making this determination should be the top priority. See page 106 of the CSA Cloud Security Guidance v4.

All the other answers may or not be elements of the incident containment process, but definitely are not the top priority.

212. Answer: D

A known-good template will be used to replace the previous workloads, if there's any suspicion that the management plane has been accessed in an unauthorized way; the customer must ensure that the new workloads have not been tampered with. See page 106 of the CSA Cloud Security Guidance v4.

Notifying law enforcement and investors, as well as other stakeholders, may be necessary, but is not typically an immediate response action. External auditors are very useful, but are not part of an incident response process.

213. Answer: D

If the incident analysis reveals that the provider was contributing to the situation that caused the incident, or the SLA was insufficient in some way, the customer may want to attempt to renegotiate the terms. See page 106 of the CSA Cloud Security Guidance v4.

The customer does not typically terminate or violate the SLA. The SLA is adopted at the outset of the cloud managed services engagement, not after an incident.

214. Answer: C, D

Continuous and serverless monitoring in the cloud may provide incident detection capabilities that are superior (in speed of detection) than traditional detection counterparts. See page 107 of the CSA Cloud Security Guidance v4.

"Oblique," "inferred," and "sentient" are not types of monitoring capabilities, and are used here only as distractors.

215. Answer: D

The chain of custody provides greater reliance on the incident data for evidentiary purposes; it is worth preserving, if possible. See page 107 of the CSA Cloud Security Guidance v4.

The chain of custody may support prosecutorial or employment actions, which is why it is so important; answers A and B are less accurate than D. Logs do not, by themselves, typically affect connections.

DOMAIN 10 ANSWERS

216. Answer: B

Cloud providers are typically operated for profit; higher security increases market shares and helps retain customers. See pages 108-109 of the CSA Cloud Security Guidance v4.

If you have a provider that is motivated by emotions, find another provider. Honor is not typically found as an incentive for provider performance. "Celebratory" has no meaning here, and is only used as a distractor.

217. Answer: A

Security measures in the cloud may be more responsive than their counterparts in the traditional environment. See page 109 of the CSA Cloud Security Guidance v4.

Physical centralization is a characteristic of the traditional environment, where cloud computing is typically distributed. Single points of failure are not benefits to a security program; they increase risk. Cloud environments are not typically homogeneous in terms of the underlying hardware, and they instead tend to be vendor neutral.

218. Answer: B

Cloud environments offer the ability to easily and inexpensively create entire distinct application stacks, such that if one were compromised by an attacker, the others would remain untouched. See page 109 of the CSA Cloud Security Guidance v4.

When cloud providers/customers span jurisdictions, this may actually create risk, not a security opportunity. Having a single set of credentials is incredibly risky, and not recommended. There is no such thing as impenetrable physical security (or impenetrable logical or digital security, for that matter).

219. Answer: C

In a traditional environment, the cost and complexity of physical hosts often results in organizations putting multiple applications/datasets on the same physical device; in the cloud, the ease of deployment and hardening, and the reduced cost of virtual machines allows the customer to deploy individual applications on single-purpose virtual machines. See page 109 of the CSA Cloud Security Guidance v4.

Regulatory capture is an undesirable situation where the regulated entity subverts the regulator. Corporate financing is not a security advantage. Internet connectivity actually poses risk to the environment.

220. Answer: A

Elasticity allows autoscaling of the cloud environment but ensuring that all newly-created workloads have the same baseline security configurations. See page 109 of the CSA Cloud Security Guidance v4.

Remote access and shared responsibilities, which are intrinsic to the cloud environment, actually pose risks, not benefits. Coercion is an undesirable situation, but the term has no meaning in this context, and is used here only as a distractor.

221. Answer: D

As a software development approach, DevOps offers opportunities for applying security early in the development process. While not unique to the cloud, DevOps is ideally suited to that environment. See page 109 of the CSA Cloud Security Guidance v4.

Waterfall and spiral are software development models that don't necessarily facilitate early inclusion of security, and are not particularly applicable to the cloud. "Angle" has no meaning in this context and is used here as a distractor.

222. Answer: B

Traditional environments are typified by administration/configuration/monitoring that requires login and management of many disparate systems, creating opportunities for human error. Cloud computing typically offers a single, simplified interface for all administrative activity, streamlining security activities. See page 109 of the CSA Cloud Security Guidance v4.

"Reverse identity" has no meaning, and is used here only as a distractor. Shared responsibilities and provider administration are actually risks associated with the cloud environment.

223. Answer: B

The cloud user will typically have less access to log data and other monitoring capabilities than in the traditional environment. See page 109 of the CSA Cloud Security Guidance v4.

Software is used in both the traditional and cloud environments; users exist in both situations, too. Cloud customer will typically have less challenge with physical security, because that is the responsibility of the provider.

224. Answer: A

The security of the management plane will directly affect the security of any and all applications in the cloud environment. See page 110 of the CSA Cloud Security Guidance v4.

Typically, the price of services are decreased and the availability of processing power is increased in the cloud environment. There are many cloud providers, and more being created every day.

225. Answer: C

Customers in a cloud environment must consider additional threat vectors/risks not normally associated with traditional IT environments, such as whatever responsibilities are assigned to the provider. See page 110 of the CSA Cloud Security Guidance v4.

"Arbitrary enforcement" has no meaning in this context, and is only used here as a distractor. Data is in binary form in both the traditional and cloud environments; files can be deleted in both, as well.

226. Answer: D

Cloud customers will typically have less insight into measures used to protect the environment, compared to the traditional environment. See page 110 of the CSA Cloud Security Guidance v4.

Reduced price is not a security challenge; it is a business opportunity. Both storage capacity and remote access capability are typically increased in the cloud environment.

227. Answer: B

This is not one of the CSA's SSDLC "meta-phases"; all the other answers are. According to these "meta-phases," testing is include in the Secure Deployment meta-phase. See page 111 of the CSA Cloud Security Guidance v4.

228. Answer: D

Cloud computing affects every aspect of the SSDLC. See page 111 of the CSA Cloud Security Guidance v4.

229. Answer: A

Reliance on an external entity (the cloud provider) will affect how developers approach software creation. See page 111 of the CSA Cloud Security Guidance v4.

OpEx versus CapEx doesn't really affect software development. Regulators do not typically dictate how software is created. There are many SSDLC frameworks for the cloud environment.

230. Answer: C

Each provider will have varying capabilities, which impacts the customer's approach to the SSDLC. See page 111 of the CSA Cloud Security

Guidance v4.

Providers definitely do not have uniform capabilities; A is incorrect. "Compliance" suggests a standard, but there are also different standards providers can use, so B is incorrect. And there is nothing on the planet that is perfect, so D is incorrect.

231. Answer: D

The management plane is a core element of the cloud environment, but not typically a part of a traditional IT environment; the management plane must be considered while trying to apply the SSDLC in the cloud. See page 111 of the CSA Cloud Security Guidance v4.

Users and external mandates are considerations in both the cloud and traditional IT environments. Price is not usually an aspect included in the SSDLC.

232. Answer: D

Organizations do not typically train regulators. All the other answers are roles within the organization that will need cloud-specific SSDLC training after migration (or, preferably, before). See page 112 of the CSA Cloud Security Guidance v4.

233. Answer: C

According to the CSA Cloud Security Guidance v4 (page 112), the deployment process is defined in the Define phase, although it might be modified later in the SSDLC.

234. Answer: D

According to the CSA Cloud Security Guidance v4 (page 112), threat modeling is applied at the Design phase of the SSDLC.

235. Answer: D

Production data should never be included in the development environment (see page 112 of the CSA Cloud Security Guidance v4), because of the risk production data may be corrupted or released.

Developers may need administrative access to the development environment and, in the cloud, that means a management plane interface. Generally, in the cloud, the development environment will be built on virtual machines.

236. Answer: B

Developers should include application logging capabilities in cloud-based applications in order to compensate for the loss of other logging sources. See page 112 of the CSA Cloud Security Guidance v4.

SIEM, DRM, and DLP are all worthwhile tools, but do not provide log data to offset the sources that may not be available in the cloud, the way application logging does.

237. Answer: D

See page 112 of the CSA Cloud Security Guidance v4.

Manual testing is less efficient and introduces greater potential for human error. "Vendor-based" testing is a misnomer if you're building your own application. Physical testing is unlikely in the cloud.

238. Answer: C

Code review is manual testing that is useful in cloud application development. See page 113 of the CSA Cloud Security Guidance v4.

Vulnerability scans and fuzz testing are usually automated tests. "Pressure testing" has no meaning in this context, and is only a distractor.

239. Answer: D, E, F

CI/CD models do not typically modify the cost of development or affect the marketability of the final product. All the other answers are benefits offered by use of a CI/CD model. See page 114 of the CSA Cloud Security Guidance v4.

240. Answer: A

DevOps supports uniformity across the organization's environments (including the development environment, the test environment, and the production environment) by using the same templates and approved code to build each environment. See page 118 of the CSA Cloud Security Guidance v4.

DevOps does not necessarily reduce costs. Users are more involved in the development process in a DevOps model than in other (more traditional) development approaches. Nothing guarantees passing an audit.

DOMAIN 11 ANSWERS

241. Answer: A, B, C, D, E

All of these are crucial data security controls in a cloud environment, according to the CSA Cloud Security Guidance v4 (see pages 119-120).

242. Answer: D

While user training may aid in securing information in the cloud, it is not a major category discussed in Domain 11 of the CSA Cloud Security Guidance v4; the other three answers are (see pages 119-120).

243. Answer: A, B, D

"Translucent" is not a data storage type; the term has no meaning in this context, and is only a distractor. All the other answers are major data storage types used in the cloud (see page 120 of the CSA Cloud Security Guidance v4).

244. Answer: C

Data dispersion is widely used in the cloud as a means to add resiliency and redundancy to data storage. See page 120 of the CSA Cloud Security Guidance v4.

Both ephemeral and RAM are temporary, not durable, storage types. "Epiphany" has no meaning here, and is only a distractor.

245. Answer: D

See page 121 of the CSA Cloud Security Guidance v4.

Firewalls are typically monitor and restrict traffic according to rules;

firewall logs might be helpful for determining what cloud services your users are utilizing, but CASB is a better answer. The purpose of SIEMs is to centralize and analyze log data; again, this might be useful for learning about user consumption of services, but CASB is still a better answer. APIs are the tools used to access and use data in the cloud; they are not designed to aid in determining usage.

246. Answer: B

Volume storage allocates a portion of storage to the customer, which the customer can use for any purpose (to include executables and entire virtual machines). See page CSA Cloud Security Guidance v4.

Object storage, as it sounds, provides a storage location in the cloud for data objects (such as files); it is typically not used as a runtime environment. CDNs are used to enhance quality of service by putting data geographically proximate to the user. SDNs are used to abstract the networking functions away from the tangible underlying hardware/connections.

247. Answer: C

Ultimately, the responsibility for which data is stored in the cloud is part of the customer's role; the customer is the organization which owns and is legally liable for the protection of the data. See page 120 of the CSA Cloud Security Guidance v4.

This is not an easy question to answer, because part of the job function of both the regulator (A) and the administrator (D) is to supervise how the customer (C) handles sensitive/controlled/regulated data, including where it is stored. However, C is still a better answer, because it is ultimately the data owner (the customer) that has the legal and ethical responsibility to protect the data. The cloud provider is not responsible for which data the customer puts into cloud storage, except under extraordinary circumstances.

248. Answer: D

Restricting which data is stored in the cloud is often an element of complying with external mandates/standards; see page 120 of the CSA Cloud Security Guidance v4.

Financial considerations might be one aspect of an organization's choice whether to store data in the cloud, but compliance is a much more crucial function. Data can generally presented in the same manner whether it is in the cloud or stored in a traditional environment; aesthetics are not typically considered when choosing where to store data. The choice of where to store data has nothing to do with training.

249. Answer: C

DLP solutions often require the ability to view the content of messaging; encryption can hinder this ability. See page 121 of the CSA Cloud Security Guidance v4.

A good DLP solution should be able to function properly under the other conditions listed.

250. Answer: D

Generally, the provider's own services will be preferable to any other option. See page 122 of the CSA Cloud Security Guidance v4.

251. Answer: B

According to the CSA, TLS is an essential security function that every cloud provider should have (see page 122 of the CSA Cloud Security Guidance v4).

The cloud provider is not responsible for the training and awareness of customers. SSL is a deprecated, earlier form of the TLS approach. DRM is a good way to add extra access control to a file, but it is not a fundamental security element.

252. Answer: A

Untrusted data should not be automatically admitted to the cloud environment. See page 122 of the CSA Cloud Security Guidance v4.

Encrypting or hashing data prior to its entry to the cloud environment does not actually serve to protect the environment. Saving the data is the same as allowing it into the environment, and is therefore not a secure practice.

253. Answer: C

According to the CSA Cloud Security Guidance v4 (page 122), these are the core data security elements in the cloud.

The other options are not core security elements, according to the CSA Cloud Security Guidance v4.

254. Answer: C

While the cloud provider should obviously secure the physical data center itself, the CSA recommendations for cloud access control for data security include only the other three answers. See page 122 of the CSA Cloud Security Guidance v4.

255. Answer: A

The default deny policy is fundamental to protecting the management plane. See page 122 of the CSA Cloud Security Guidance v4.

Default delete and overwrite are not real approaches to either operations or security, as they would create a situation where data is constantly being destroyed. Default allow would be a very permissive situation, and would result in frequent unauthorized access to the cloud environment.

256. Answer: D

It is preferable that the customer manage their own keys, in order to reduce potential for exposure. See page 128 of the CSA Cloud Security Guidance v4.

While AES is a widely accepted encryption standard, CSA does not recommend any particular encryption scheme. Similarly, symmetric is a useful encryption method, but asymmetric is also useful. There is no such thing as one-way encryption; in order for encryption to be useful, it must be reversible.

257. Answer: B

Customers should consider building security into the architecture of the cloud environment to promote data security. See page 128 of the CSA Cloud Security Guidance v4.

User training is also a very useful tool, but probably not as effective as secure architecture techniques. "Inverse proportions" has no meaning in this context, and is only used here as a distractor. The cloud customer has no means to apply physical security controls to the cloud environment.

258. Answer: D

Because the test environment utilizes systems/applications that have not been fully tested, and therefore may not be secure, raw production data should not be included there. See page 127 of the CSA Cloud Security Guidance v4.

New systems and code currently under development are exactly the elements that should be in a test environment. Security can (and should) also be applied to the test environment.

259. Answer: B

Certain features in a cloud environment might not be able to process encrypted data (like files under a DRM scheme), and may therefore not work properly. See page 127 of the CSA Cloud Security Guidance v4.

DRM does not rely on user awareness, creativity, or administrative rights.

260. Answer: D

Data centers are not the typical place to install DLP solutions; instead, they are usually placed at locations accessible to users (endpoints, servers, etc.). See page 126 of the CSA Cloud Security Guidance v4.

DLP solutions can be placed in remote locations, commercial websites, and the cloud.

261. Answer: C

Logs must be stored securely, to ensure integrity. This might include the cloud, an on-prem option, or underground bunkers; B is the best answer because it includes the others. See page 126 of the CSA Cloud Security Guidance v4.

262. Answer: C

A government disclosure order may force the provider to disclose either the keys or the data (or both). See page 126 of the CSA Cloud Security Guidance v4.

Oddly, this is one situation where users are prevented from creating problems; the user does not typically have direct access to the keys, and could not therefore expose them. In both misconfiguration and failure of physical systems, it is much more likely that all access will be prevented (fail secure) instead of the keys being exposed.

263. Answer: D

Regulators do not typically store encryption keys for the entities they oversee. All the other answers are encryption key management options. See page 125 of the CSA Cloud Security Guidance v4.

264. Answer: D

The main considerations of key management in the cloud are performance, latency, security, and accessibility. See page 125 of the CSA Cloud Security Guidance v4.

265. Answer: C

According to the CSA Cloud Security Guidance v4 (page 124), object storage used for application back-ends should be encrypted by engines in the client or application itself.

"Cloud" is too general an answer to be correct. CSA does not recommend the engine be located on specific hardware devices, probably because the cloud requires more flexibility, as customer instances will be spread across many devices. We typically don't locate encryption engines on portable devices.

DOMAIN 12 ANSWERS

266. Answer: B

Unlike in traditional IT environments, no single party solely manages IAM in the cloud; instead, the provider and customer must share the responsibility and implementation. See page 129 of the CSA Cloud Security Guidance v4.

267. Answer: B

While the legal framework will almost certainly inform the shared IAM responsibilities between the customer and provider, the other three answers are included in all cloud relationships. See page 129 of the CSA Cloud Security Guidance v4.

268. Answer: C

Identity federation allows multiple organizations/providers to share identity and access control. See page 130 of the CSA Cloud Security Guidance v4.

DRM is used to create an additional layer of access control to objects/files; DLP is egress monitoring. Virtualization is used to share resources across multiple users, not for sharing identity information.

269. Answer: B

This is the definition of authentication. See page 131 of the CSA Cloud Security Guidance v4.

270. Answer: D

Passwords are commonly used as authentication factors. See page 131 of the CSA Cloud Security Guidance v4. None of the other answers provide authentication.

271. Answer: D

The identity assertion must be unique for every entity, so that each entity can be granted appropriate access rights. See page 131 of the CSA Cloud Security Guidance v4.

Identity assertions do not have to be kept secret; in fact, they are often publicized (such as email addresses). Nor do they have to be shared. "Neglected" has no meaning in this context, and is only a distractor.

272. Answer: A

SAML is based on XML, created by OASIS, an open standard consortium. See page 132 of the CSA Cloud Security Guidance v4.

CANT does not exist; I made it up as a distractor for this question. Linux is an operating system. REST is a design approach for creating application programming interfaces (APIs).

273. Answer: B

There is no reverse party in SAML; this is only a distractor, as the term has no meaning. See page 132 of the CSA Cloud Security Guidance v4.

All the other answers are SAML elements. I highly, highly recommend the Wikipedia entry for SAML, which is incredibly detailed and extensive.

274. Answer: C

See page 132.

275. Answer: D

See page 132 of the CSA Cloud Security Guidance v4.

276. Answer: A

This describes OpenID Connect. See page 132 of the CSA Cloud Security Guidance v4.

Answer B is a Star Trek reference, used here as a distractor. SOAP is a design protocol for application programming interfaces (APIs). TCP/IP is a networking communications protocol.

277. Answer: D

Manually managing identities is difficult for organizations of any appreciable size. See page 134 of the CSA Cloud Security Guidance v4.

Modern major cloud providers should have little difficulty providing necessary amounts of processing and storage capacity for most customers. Identity management should not require memorization.

278. Answer: C, D

See page 136. While A and B are very useful for cloud security, they're not essential to IAM efforts. While E and F may aid IAM efforts, they are very specific technologies, where C and D are foundational approaches.

279. Answer: B

An entitlement matrix helps the data owner ascribe permissions to specific entities under particular conditions. See page 138 of the CSA Cloud Security Guidance v4.

A and C are only distractors; these are terms with no meaning in our industry. DRM is used to add an extra layer of access control on files/objects.

280. Answer: B

The cloud customer will define permissions and grant authorizations, but the provider will be responsible for enforcing these. See page 138 of the CSA Cloud Security Guidance v4.

DOMAIN 13 ANSWERS

281. Answer: D

According to the CSA Cloud Security Guidance v4 (page 140), a technology must be delivered as a cloud service in order to be considered SecaaS.

The technology does not have to exist inside a single jurisdiction, service cloud customers, or be certified according to the STAR program in order to be considered SecaaS.

282. Answer: A

According to the CSA Cloud Security Guidance v4 (page 140), a technology must be satisfy the NIST defintion of a cloud service in order to be considered SecaaS.

The technology does not have to use VPNs or TLS, or satisfy GDPR in order to be considered SecaaS.

283. Answer: B

Data leakage is a potential risk associated with SecaaS, not a potential benefit. See page 141-142 of the CSA Cloud Security Guidance v4.

284. Answer: D and E

The challenge of changing providers and migrating to a cloud security provider are potential concerns associated with SecaaS, not potential benefits. See pages 141-142 of the CSA Cloud Security Guidance v4.

285. Answer: A

Cloud customers might exist across many different jurisdictions, each with their own regulatory restrictions; it is difficult for a single provider to meet the needs of every customer on the planet. See page 142 of the CSA Cloud Security Guidance v4.

Price, education, and the emotions of regulators are not usually limiting factors.

286. Answer: B

"CASB" is a term describing a cloud security gateway. See page 143 of the CSA Cloud Security Guidance v4.

The STAR Registry is a list of STAR-compliant providers; the CCM is a table of controls mapped against regulations and standards; and the GDPR is a European law.

287. Answer: C

Federated identity brokers manage identity and access management in the cloud. See page 142 of the CSA Cloud Security Guidance v4.

Transparent encryption is a technique applied to databases. Type 2 hypervisors manage virtual machines. Remote meetings are not a security service.

288. Answer: D

See page 143 of the CSA Cloud Security Guidance v4.

User training is not typically considered an SecaaS offering. AES is an encryption standard, not a technology/service. A flotation device is used for water safety.

289. Answer: A

See page143 of the CSA Cloud Security Guidance v4.

Deep packet inspection and heuristic algorithms are typically elements of a firewall or IDS/IPS device. The Turing test is used to determine whether artificial intelligence can approximate human responses-- this is not part of the CCSK exam or the information security industry.

290. Answer: B and E

SecaaS vendors should not be offering financial or legal consulting; those are typically areas best handled by accountants/auditors and attorneys. All the other answers are services offered by SecaaS providers. See pages 144-145 of the CSA Cloud Security Guidance v4.

DOMAIN 14 ANSWERS

291. Answer: B

"Distributed billing" is a nonsense term used here only as a distractor. All the other answers are common characteristics of big data solutions. See page 147 of the CSA Cloud Security Guidance v4.

292. Answer: D

The chance of human error is not particularly elevated by the use of IoT solutions. See page 149 of the CSA Cloud Security Guidance v4.

293. Answer: A

Device registration, authentication, and authorization are processes that must be done correctly and uniformly for each device in order to properly protect the enterprise. Doing this is a significant challenge. See page 149 of the CSA Cloud Security Guidance v4.

Office politics, candidate screening, and job rotation are not issues that may affect the security of mobile devices connected to the cloud.

294. Answer: B

DLP agents are among the list of services typically considered as "serverless" in the CSA Cloud Security Guidance v4, page 150.

295. Answer: B

In a serverless architecture, almost the entire application stack runs in the provider's environment, without any input or control by the customer. See page 150 of the CSA Cloud Security Guidance v4.

The cloud architecture should not affect the security responsibilities of the regulator or customer, regardless of which kind of architecture is utilized.

CLOUD CONTROLS MATRIX (CCM) ANSWERS

296. Answer: D

The BCR Domain in the CCM includes data backup and recovery controls. See BCR-01 in the CCM.

297. Answer: B

The CCC Domain addresses elements of the ITIL Service Management requirements. See CCC-02 and CCC-03 in the CCM.

298. Answer: C

GRM-05 in the CCM specifically addresses senior management's commitment to the information security program.

299. Answer: B

HRS-07 in the CCM specifically addresses the roles and responsibilities of employees, contractors, and third parties.

300. Answer: C

IAM-02, IAM-06, IAM-08, and IAM-10 in the CCM specifically address the concept of least privilege. Least privilege is also mentioned in the Infrastructure and Virtualization Domain, but this was not one of the options listed.

301. Answer: A

MOS-03 requires the cloud environment to be governed by a policy limiting the use of non-approved applications or applications from untrusted sources.

WPA2 is not a control in the CCM; it is a wireless security standard.

302. Answer: D

303. Answer: B

Policies addressing encryption key generation are mentioned in EKM-02.

304. Answer: F

305. Answer: A, B, C, D, E, F

IAM-11 applies to all architectures.

306. Answer: C

IVS-07 applies to the Compute architecture.

307. Answer: D

SEF-05 applies to all types of cloud service models.

308. Answer: A

IVS-02 applies to the IaaS model.

309. Answer: A

IVS-05 is the responsibility of the provider. Regulators and taxpayers are generally outside the scope of cloud security responsibility.

310. Answer: D

IVS-07 is the responsibility of both the cloud provider and the customer.

311. Answer: C, D

FERPA is a US federal law that applies to academic providers. HIPAA is a US federal law that applies to medical providers.

PIPEDA is a Canadian law. COPPA is a US law that only applies to minors. GDPR is a European law. ENISA is a European standards body.

312. Answer: C, D, E

BSI is a German privacy law. GDPR is a European privacy law. PCI DSS is a contractual standard for processing payment card information.

NERC CIP is a US law for electrical power providers. NIST SP 800-53 is applicable to US federal government agencies.

313. Answer: A, B

COBIT and ISO are both international standards, often used in industrial settings.

FERPA and HIPAA are both only applicable to US entities in specific sectors. GDPR is a European privacy law.

314. Answer: C

PIPEDA is a Canadian privacy law.

HIPAA, ITAR, and NERC CIP are only applicable to US entities. NZISM is only applicable to entities in New Zealand.

ENISA CLOUD COMPUTING ANSWERS

315. Answer: D

According to the ENISA Cloud Computing: Benefits, Risks, and Recommendations for Information Security (page 4), cloud computing's economies of scale and flexibility are "both a friend and a foe from a security point of view."

316. Answer: C

According to the ENISA Cloud Computing: Benefits, Risks, and Recommendations for Information Security (pages 7-8), all the answers except for D are top security benefits of the cloud.

317. Answer: B

According to the ENISA Cloud Computing: Benefits, Risks, and Recommendations for Information Security (pages 9-10), all of the answers except for B are top security risks associated with cloud computing. This is a nuanced question, because "malicious insiders" is one of the top security risks listed in the ENISA document. The crucial difference between the answer listed and the element listed in the ENISA guidance is malice versus error; the intent of the person involved.

318. Answer: A

See page 25 of the ENISA Cloud Computing: Benefits, Risks, and Recommendations for Information Security.

319. Answer: A

HIPAA is a US federal law that applies to medical providers and their business associates; all the other answers are software security standards mentioned in the ENISA Cloud Computing: Benefits, Risks, and Recommendations for Information Security (see page 73).

320. Answer: A

According to the ENISA Cloud Computing: Benefits, Risks, and Recommendations for Information Security, attacks on cloud resource isolation mechanisms is more difficult and less common than attacking traditional OSs (see page 9 of that document). Therefore, A is correct, and B and C are incorrect.

Attacks on both occur constantly, so D is incorrect.

321. Answer: B

Cache poisoning is not one of the types of attacks listed in the ENISA Cloud Computing: Benefits, Risks, and Recommendations for Information Security entry on economic denial of service (see page 41). All the other answers are listed in that entry.

322. Answer: B

Typically, the software is the asset being licensed, not something affected by failure to properly license it. All the other answers are assets affected by licensing risks. See page 47 of the ENISA Cloud Computing: Benefits, Risks, and Recommendations for Information Security.

323. Answer: D

This is the definition of VM hopping, from the ENISA Cloud Computing: Benefits, Risks, and Recommendations for Information Security, page 54.

324. Answer: B

User training is a security issue, but not necessarily a legal issue associated with cloud computing. See page 97 of the ENISA Cloud

Computing: Benefits, Risks, and Recommendations for Information Security.

325. Answer: B

The ENISA Cloud Computing: Benefits, Risks, and Recommendations for Information Security (page 27) recommends using standards such as OVF to ease cloud migrations.

Each of the other answers does not help with portability, and may, in fact, make migration more difficult.

326. Answer: B

The cloud customer is typically the data controller. See page 66 of the ENISA Cloud Computing: Benefits, Risks, and Recommendations for Information Security.

327. Answer: A

The cloud provider is typically the data processor. See page 66 of the ENISA Cloud Computing: Benefits, Risks, and Recommendations for Information Security.

328. Answer: D

See page 68 of the ENISA Cloud Computing: Benefits, Risks, and Recommendations for Information Security.

329. Answer: C

According to the the ENISA Cloud Computing: Benefits, Risks, and Recommendations for Information Security (page 42), internal probes are one of the underlying vulnerabilities related to malicious probes/scans.

All the other answers are not included in the list of underlying vulnerabilities for that risk in that document.